The Expository Pulpit Series

1-2 PETER

A Holy Walk In

A Hostile World

by

Dr. Glen Spencer Jr.

SPENCER'S EVANGELISTIC MINISTRIES
15 Pine Ridge Road – Tunkhannock, Pa. 18657
EMAIL: GraceForLiving@epix.net

1-2 Peter: A Holy Walk In A Hostile World
Copyright © 2008 by Glen Spencer Jr.

All Rights Reserved. No part of this book may be reproduced, stored in a retrieval system or transmitted in any form by any means, electronic, mechanical, photocopy, recording, or otherwise, without the prior permission of the author, except as provided by USA copyright law.

All Scripture Quotations From The King James Bible

Contents

1 PETER

Strange And Scattered 7
A Living Hope In A Dying World 15
A Plea For Holy Living 23
Our Great Redemption 31
It's Time To grow Up 43
Building On The Rock 49
Christian Living In A Wicked World........................55
Christian Citizenship 61
When Life Isn't Fair..67
The Wife Who Wins Her Husband 75
The Husband Who Wins His Wife 81
Living The Good Life 87
How To Be Used Of God 95
The Triumphant Christ...101
Living In The Shadow Of Eternity..........................115
How To Survive Your Trials 131
The Pastoral Ministry..139
Getting Ahead In The Christian Life 149
You Better Be Careful Out There 153

2 PETER

How To Have A Fall Proof Life................................163
Why The Preacher Repeats Himself 171
A More Sure Word..177
False Teachers 183
God's Judgment On False Teachers.......................189

The Consequences Of Heresy	195
Empty Wells, Vomiting Dogs And Wallowing Hogs	203
End Time Scoffers	211
God Is Never Late	221
According To His Promise	231

Recommendations From Our Readers

Pastor Spencer is not only a gifted preacher, but a gifted writer as well. As a fundamentalist and pastor, I am careful about the books I endorse, but Dr. Spencer is at the top of my list of writers. So, it is with great honor that I recommend his Expository Pulpit Series to you.

Michael D. McClary, Th.D,
Pastor, Community-Bainbridge Baptist Church,
Founder/Executive Director, Good Samaritan Ministries

I have enjoyed reading your books in the past and look forward to getting newer ones. The thing I enjoyed about your books were that when I read them I said, "I have to teach this to my people. I want others to know this". I appreciate your study, work and insight.

Dr. Jeff Fugate
Pastor, Clays Mill Road Baptist Church
President of Commonwealth Baptist College

Dr. Glen Spencer's Bible commentaries are valuable for today. They are expository, edifying and exciting in aiding the Christian, the teacher and the preacher to understand the mind of God and to become victorious in their daily lives. I will use the complete set.

Dr. Bruce Miller, Evangelist
President of Atlantic Coast Baptist College

It is with great delight that I recommend to you, "The Expository Pulpit Commentary Series." Dr. Glen Spencer Jr. combines years of exhaustive research and practical ministry experience to bring to the church, the pastor, the teacher, and the student of the Scriptures a sound, in-depth and yet very practical set of study tools. This ongoing verse by commentary series will be a great addition to your library. This is not just more rehashed information but wise insight from a seasoned Bible Scholar. I know Dr. Glen Spencer Jr. the man and have found him to be a great Christian, a compassionate pastor and a true champion of the authorized King James Bible, believing it to be God's Preserved Word For English speaking people.

This trustworthy commentary series is, Dispensational in theology, pre-Tribulation and pre-millennial in its eschatology, literal in its hermeneutical approach and expository in its format. I am thrilled that this good work is now available to you and I as we seek to benefit from its invaluable help to deepen our knowledge of God's perfect, preserved word.

Dr. Jon M. Jenkins,
Pastor, Grace Baptist Church
President of Grace Baptist College

"You have written an excellent study on the Book of Revelation. This will be a great help to preachers and teachers everywhere. This work is informative, inspiring, and encouraging. Your alliterative outlines are excellent! Your study of this book will be a great help to many, many Christians."

Dr. Lee Roberson
Founder of Tennessee Temple University

Strange And Scattered
1 Peter 1:1-2

The little book of 1 Peter is a letter of help, hope and holiness. The Apostle Peter instructs his readers on how to have a holy walk in a hostile world. He encourages those who are suffering for Christ to stay on course and forge ahead in spite of the opposition. Even in such trying times, God's people are to press on. In the first two verses Peter gets right to the heart of the matter explaining that God's people are pilgrims passing through this world.

GOD'S PEOPLE ARE STRANGERS

Peter, an apostle of Jesus Christ, to the strangers.... (1 Peter 1:1) Notice that we are called **strangers.** This word stranger speaks of one who is a "*pilgrim or foreigner.*" This is a very descriptive term of what every believer is. We are foreigners to this world. This world is not our home, we are mere strangers to here. The songwriter wrote:

This world is not my home, I'm just passing through.
My treasures are laid up, Somewhere beyond the blue.
The angels beckon me, From Heaven's open door,
And I can't be at home, In this world anymore.

As God's people we are in the world, but not of the world. Jesus said, **I have chosen you out of the world. (John 15:19)** Notice the words **out of.** When we became Christ's we ceased to be of this world. When we were saved we became citizens of another country. Our real citizenship is in Heaven

> **For our conversation is in heaven; from whence also we look for the Saviour, the Lord Jesus Christ: (Philippians 3:20)**
>
> **For we know that if our earthly house of this tabernacle were dissolved, we have a building of God, an house not made with hands, eternal in the heavens. (2 Corinthians 5:1)**

That is why we are admonished, **Love not the world, neither the things that are in the world. If any man love the world, the love of the Father is not in him. (1 John 2:15)** We are told to **come out from among them, and be ye separate, saith the Lord, and touch not the unclean thing. (2 Corinthians 6:17)** By way of the new birth we are creatures of another world. **For here have we no continuing city, but we seek one to come. (Hebrews 13:14)**

GOD'S PEOPLE ARE SCATTERED

Peter, an apostle of Jesus Christ, to the strangers scattered .... (1 Peter 1:1) Not only are we strangers, we are **scattered.** The word **scattered** comes from the word *diaspora* and carries the idea of *that which is sown.* It was a word used of the farmer sowing seed in the field. The *dispersion* was a term understood by Jews to mean all the Jews who had been scattered abroad through persecution. In the context Peter is writing to the Jews who were **scattered throughout Pontus, Galatia, Cappadocia, Asia, and Bithynia.** These were all provinces of Asia Minor. But it doesn't matter whether it is Pontus or Pennsylvania, Galatia or Georgia, Cappadocia or California, Asia or Alabama, Bithynia or Birmingham, like a farmer sows seed in his field, the Lord sows Christians throughout the fields of this world. In the book of Acts God allowed persecution to scatter His people for purpose of spreading the good news of the gospel. Every believer is in a specific place for a specific ministry. Think about it! You are where you are because God has put you there to spread the gospel.

GOD'S PEOPLE ARE SELECTED

As God's people we are **Elect according to the foreknowledge of God the Father. (1 Peter 1:2a)** Here is a subject that is the spring board for a great deal of controversy. However, we must keep in mind that God's election cannot be divorced from His foreknowledge. The foreknowledge of God is the basis for His election. God is timeless. Based upon anything except God's foreknowledge, election would be fatalistic, depriving man of his free choice which the Bible commands him to exercise. If we are going to understand how God elects man we are going to have to accept what the Bible says about God's foreknowledge.

Notice the Holy Spirit inspired order of foreknowledge and election. **Elect according to the foreknowledge of God.** Now don't get this out of order. Some attempt to teach that God foreknew the elect because He had pre-selected them to be saved. However, we see that election is according to foreknowledge. It does not say, *Foreknowledge according to His election.* NO! A thousand times NO! Let's just be honest and read the Bible as God wrote it. The Bible makes it clear that God's election is based upon His foreknowledge.

Foreknowledge is the act whereby God, based upon His omniscience, looked down through the ages and seeing who would come to Christ and be saved, He therefore, elected them and predestined them to be conformed to the image of Christ.

GOD'S PEOPLE ARE SANCTIFIED

Through sanctification of the Spirit unto obedience. (1 Peter 1:2b) The word *"sanctify"* means *"to be set apart for special service."* The text says that this sanctifying work is accomplished by the Holy Spirit. The sanctifying work of the Holy Spirit is that act whereby He works in the life of the believer to free him from the world, the flesh, and the devil while at the same time separating him unto Christ for special service. As we study the Scriptures we learn that the doctrine of sanctification involves a three-fold work.

Positional Sanctification

This speaks of our position in Christ. At the time of the new birth, every believer is eternally sanctified in Christ and transferred from the family of the devil into the family of God. At the very moment of salvation we become a child of God.

> **But as many as received him, to them gave he power to become the sons of God, even to them that believe on his name. (John 1:12)**

Before salvation we belonged to the devil—we were subjects of his kingdom. Jesus said to the unsaved, **Ye are of your father the devil... (John 8:44)** However, salvation changed everything and now we are subjects of the kingdom of God.

> **Giving thanks unto the Father, which hath made us meet to be partakers of the inheritance of the saints in light: Who hath delivered us from the power of darkness, and hath translated us into the kingdom of his dear Son. (Colossians 1:12-13)**

At that moment God declared us perfectly righteous and set us apart for Himself. This is positional sanctification that takes place the minute one is saved. It is the act of God whereby **Christ is made unto us ... sanctification. (1 Corinthians 1:30)** This phase of sanctification is solely the work of God.

Progressive Sanctification

It differs from Positional sanctification in that positional sanctification is entirely the work of God while progressive sanctification includes human responsibility. Progressive sanctification is the process of being conformed to the image of Christ. (Romans 8:29) This is Christian growth, putting away sin and putting on godliness.

> **I speak after the manner of men because of the infirmity of your flesh: for as ye have yielded your members servants to uncleanness and to iniquity unto iniquity; even so now yield your members servants to righteousness unto holiness. (Romans 6:19)**

> **But now being made free from sin, and become servants to God, ye have your fruit unto holiness, and the end everlasting life. Romans 6:22**

All believers are exhorted to pursue Sanctification.

For this is the will of God, even your sanctification, that ye should abstain from fornication. (1 Thessalonians 4:3)

This aspect of our sanctification is a matter of choice to the believer.

If a man therefore purge himself from these, he shall be a vessel unto honour, sanctified, and meet for the master's use, and prepared unto every good work. Flee also youthful lusts: but follow righteousness, faith, charity, peace, with them that call on the Lord out of a pure heart. (2 Timothy 2:21-22)

Unfortunately, the choice of many Christians is to ignore God's clear command to separate and they never become **a vessel unto honour, sanctified, and meet for the master's use.** God intends that the process of sanctification continue throughout the believer's life. This present process of sanctification never ends as far as this life is concerned. The Christian is to combat and resist sin until he is taken from this world at death or at the return of Christ.

Perfect Sanctification

It is the final perfection of the believer which will take place at the return of Christ. **And the very God of peace sanctify you wholly; and I pray God your whole spirit and soul and body be preserved blameless unto the coming of our Lord Jesus Christ. (1 Thessalonians 5:23)** Perfect sanctification is the plan and purpose of God for every believer. This phase of sanctification cannot and will not be attained while in our mortal bodies. However, it will be accomplished—what God started in the believer, He will finish.

Being confident of this very thing, that he which hath begun a good work in you will perform it until the day of Jesus Christ. (Philippians 1:6)

Perfect sanctification will be the completion of what God started in us on the day of our salvation. Like positional sanctification, this is wholly the work of God. At Christ's coming, every believer will receive a new body that will have no sin. **Beloved, now are we the sons of God, and it doth not yet appear what we shall be: but we know that, when he shall appear, we shall be like him; for we shall see him as he is. (1 John 3:2)** The Christian will no longer have to resist sin within or to grow toward perfection. His sanctification will be complete. He will be wholly and forever set apart to God from sin.

GOD'S PEOPLE ARE SUBMISSIVE

Unto obedience and sprinkling of the blood of Jesus Christ: Grace unto you, and peace, be multiplied. (1 Peter 1:2c) Notice that this sanctifying work is **unto obedience.** God's people are to obey the Holy Spirit and put away sin as the Spirit of God convicts. That's obedience.

Next, Peter speaks of **sprinkling of the blood of Jesus Christ.** Many interpret this to mean the cleansing by the blood that takes place the moment a sinner gets saved. The blood of Christ is certainly the basis of our forgiveness. However, that's not what Peter is saying here. You will notice that this blood is sprinkled after the sanctifying work of the Holy Spirit and after obedience to Christ, not before it. This is speaking of the continual cleansing of the blood of Christ in our life. John said, **If we confess our sins, he is faithful and just to forgive us our sins, and to cleanse us from all unrighteousness. (1 John 1:9)** Confession comes from a word that means "*to speak the same thing,* It carries the idea of *agreeing with another.* "Confession is agreeing what God says about sin.

When David confession his sin of adultery he said, **Against thee, thee only, have I sinned, and done this evil in thy sight: that thou mightest be justified when thou speakest, and be clear when thou judgest. (Psalm 51:4)** It might also be noted that the word confess is in the present tense, denoting the need for continuous confessing. Notice that the cleansing is conditional upon the confessing. When confession is right it will result in cleansing. Solomon dealt with this matter of sin along with the confession and cleansing of it. **He that covereth his sins shall not prosper: but whoso confesseth and forsaketh them shall have mercy. (Proverbs 28:13)** When the Holy Spirit is active in a person's life sanctification will be the result.

A Living Hope In A Dying World
1 Peter 1:3-9

The Bible often refers to the salvation experience as a hope. Paul speaking of believers who had died, said we **sorrow not, even as others which have no hope. (1 Thessalonians 4:13)** Concerning the Christian the Bible speaks of, **the hope of his calling. (Ephesians 1:18)** Of every child of God the Bible says, **Christ in you, the hope of glory. (Colossians 1:27)** Here in 1 Peter our text states that **God according to his abundant mercy has begotten us again unto a lively hope. (1 Peter 1:3)** The salvation experience is referred to as **hope.** Now there is a big difference between the way we generally use the word **hope** and the way the Bible uses it. When we use the word hope, it is in the sense of *"wishing for something."* However, when the Bible uses that word hope, it is talking about a *"confident expectation and reality."* The reason that Bible hope is a confident expectation and reality is because Bible hope is based in God.

> **Now the God of hope fill you with all joy and peace in believing, that ye may abound in hope, through the power of the Holy Ghost. (Romans 15:13)**

Paul calls God **the God of hope.** Bible hope has its foundation in God. When we talk about our salvation being a **lively hope,** we're not just wishing for Heaven, we have a *"confident expectation"* of Heaven. In this passage Peter speaks of our **lively hope.** We have a Living Hope In A Dying World.

THE REGENERATION OF OUR SOUL

Blessed be the God and Father of our Lord Jesus Christ, which according to his abundant mercy hath begotten us again unto a lively hope .... (1 Peter 1:3a) The phrase **begotten us again** means that we have been born again. Jesus said, **Verily, verily, I say unto thee, Except a man be born again, he cannot see the kingdom of God. (John 3:3)** We sometimes hear folks scoff at this wonderful Bible phrase. I have talked to people about their souls who immediately object by pointing out folks who claim to be born again, but never change. The Bible says, **Therefore if any man be in Christ, he is a new creature: old things are passed away; behold, all things are become new. (2 Corinthians 5:17)** The term born again is a good Bible term and believers need not shy away from it just because the world doesn't like it. But one thing is for sure. Being born again means a changed life. When a baby is born a new life enters the world. The same is true of the spiritual birth. When a sinner turns from his sin to Jesus Christ as his personal Savior, a new life enters the world. Salvation is not business as usual. We have a living hope in a dying world because of the Regeneration Of Our Soul.

THE RESURRECTION OF OUR SAVIOUR

This hope is based upon **the resurrection of Jesus Christ from the dead. (1 Peter 1:3)** Notice that our hope is dependent on the resurrection of Christ. There would be no Christianity if there were no resurrection. Paul wrote, **And if**

Christ be not raised, your faith is vain; ye are yet in your sins. Then they also which are fallen asleep in Christ are perished. If in this life only we have hope in Christ, we are of all men most miserable. (1 Corinthians 15:17-19) Praise God. Christianity has a living Saviour. If Christ had remained in the tomb, we would have no hope. Oliver B. Greene said, *"The greatest bombshell ever to explode in the face of an unbelieving world was the bodily resurrection of Jesus Christ."* The resurrection of Jesus distinguishes and makes Christianity superior to all other religions of the world. Founders of Religions have lived and died and they remain dead. But Jesus Christ the founder of New Testament Christianity died and yet He is alive. You can go to the grave of Mary Baker Eddy, the founder of Christian Science and there she lies. You can go to the grave of Charles Taze Russell, the founder of the Jehovah's Witness and there he lies. You can go to the grave of Joseph Smith, the founder of Mormonism and there he lies. You can go to the grave of Mohammed, the founder of Islam and there he lies. But you go to Joseph's tomb where they lay Jesus dead and He is not there. There is no religion other than Christianity that can point to an empty tomb and say, **He is risen, He is not here. (Mark 16:6)** The resurrection of Christ is the bedrock upon which Christianity sits.

THE RESERVING OF OUR SALVATION

To an inheritance incorruptible, and undefiled, and that fadeth not away, reserved in heaven for you. (1 Peter 1:4) The verse speaks of our **inheritance.** An **inheritance** is wealth that one receives as a member of a family. We already have the **earnest of our inheritance (Ephesians**

1:14), which is the Holy Spirit. (2 Corinthians 1:22, 5:5) The word earnest speaks of *a pledge of a part given in advance.* The Holy Spirit is the Divine pledge of our future inheritance. Furthermore, the Bible calls us **joint-heirs with Christ. (Romans 8:17)** As joint-heirs we share in everything that Jesus Christ inherits. Peter uses three words to describe the surety of the believer's inheritance.

Our inheritance will not Decay

The word **incorruptible** means that our inheritance is not subject to decay. Thayer defines it as *"not liable to corruption or decay, imperishable."* Our inheritance will not spoil and waste away.

Our inheritance will not become Defiled

The word **undefiled** speaks of "*being unstained or un-polluted."* Our inheritance is pure and will remain pure. This same word is used to speak of the purity of Christ. **For such an high priest became us, who is holy, harmless, undefiled, separate from sinners, and made higher than the heavens. (Hebrews 7:26)**

Our an inheritance will not Dull

We are assured that our inheritance **fadeth not away.** This phrase was used to describe a flower that did not wither or die. Instead it maintained its beauty and fragrance. Our inheritance will never lose its splendor. Its splendor and beauty will shine throughout the endless ages of eternity.

Peter assures us that this inheritance is **reserved in heaven for you.** The word **reserved** is a military term that speaks of something being *watched over* or *guarded.*

Kenneth Wuest said, *"Heaven is the safe-deposit box where God is guarding our inheritance for us under constant surveillance."* No wonder Jesus said, **Lay not up for yourselves treasures upon earth, where moth and rust doth corrupt, and where thieves break through and steal: But lay up for yourselves treasures in heaven, where neither moth nor rust doth corrupt, and where thieves do not break through nor steal. (Matthew 6:19-20)**

Who are kept by the power of God through faith unto salvation ready to be revealed in the last time. (1 Peter 1:5) Our eternal security rests in God's power to keep us. That is real security. (see Romans 8:31–39) As long as the believer's security is dependent on God we will get to Heaven. **Now unto him that is able to keep you from falling, and to present you faultless before the presence of his glory with exceeding joy. (Jude 1:24)** As believers in Christ our salvation is the surest thing we have. Jesus said, **All that the Father giveth me shall come to me; and him that cometh to me I will in no wise cast out. (John 6:37)** A little later our Lord said, **And I give unto them eternal life; and they shall never perish, neither shall any man pluck them out of my hand. (John 10:28)**

THE REJOICING IN OUR SORROW

Wherein ye greatly rejoice, though now for a season, if need be, ye are in heaviness through manifold temptations. (1 Peter 1:6) Folks don't usually put rejoicing and sorrow together, but when you are a Christian things are different. Notice that the believer doesn't simply rejoice, but he can **greatly rejoice.** We can greatly rejoice though experiencing **manifold temptations.** The word manifold means *various* or *different kinds.* The idea is that no matter what comes at us we can still rejoice. Peter wrote this during some of the most horrifying persecution that God's people have ever faced. These words were written during the rule of the wicked Roman emperor Nero. Nero hated Christ and Christianity with a passion. During these times Christians were dipped in tar and set on fire as human torches to light Nero's gardens at night. Christians were wrapped in freshly slaughtered animal skins and fed to dogs and wild animals. Believers were dropped into caldrons of boiling oil. It was during this time of persecution that Peter himself was put to death.

Toward the end of this book Peter writes, **But the God of all grace, who hath called us unto his eternal glory by Christ Jesus, after that ye have suffered a while, make you perfect, stablish, strengthen, settle you. (1 Peter 5:10)** Did you pick up on the phrase **after that ye have suffered a while.** Our focus is not on the here and now, but what comes **after.** We can **greatly rejoice** in these **manifold temptations** because we know that it is only for **a while.** Suffering here is brief when compared to our inheritance that lasts for all eternity.

THE REASON FOR OUR SUFFERING

That the trial of your faith, being much more precious than of gold that perisheth, though it be tried with fire. (1 Peter 1:7a) Peter uses the analogy here of gold being refined by fire. For raw gold to be purified it must be melted and the dross skimmed off. In order to do that the gold must be heated to 1,900 degrees Fahrenheit. Once the gold is melted, the impurities rise to the surface, where they are skimmed off. God does the same thing with our faith. He allows our faith to enter into the fire. He allows these trials and afflictions into our lives for the purpose of burning off the impurities and leaving us with pure, genuine faith.

THE RETURN OF OUR SAVIOUR

Peter continues, **though it be tried with fire, might be found unto praise and honour and glory at the appearing of Jesus Christ: Whom having not seen, ye love; in whom, though now ye see him not, yet believing, ye rejoice with joy unspeakable and full of glory: Receiving the end of your faith, even the salvation of your souls. (1 Peter 1:7b-9)** Here is our blessed hope. The Bible says that we, **might be found unto praise and honour and glory at the appearing of Jesus Christ.** This is the day that every faithful believer longs for. Paul admonished us to be, **Looking for that blessed hope, and the glorious appearing of the great God and our Saviour Jesus Christ. (Titus 2:13)** Notice the phrase **looking for**. This and many other passages teach the imminent return of Christ. The word imminent means *"impending or looming."* Concerning the rapture, it means the Church could be caught out immediately or at any moment. The Scriptures continually admonish believers to **watch, be ready,** and to expect His return **at a time when ye think not.** This imminent return was the hope of the early Church. Their popular greeting, **Maranatha (1 Corinthians 16:22),** expressed their belief in the imminent return of Christ for the Church. Paul wrote, **For the Lord himself shall**

descend from heaven with a shout, with the voice of the archangel, and with the trump of God; and the dead in Christ shall rise first; Then we which are alive and remain shall be caught up together with them in the clouds, to meet the Lord in the air: and so shall we ever be with the Lord. (1 Thessalonians 4:16-17) The rapture is the next great event in the redemptive plan and purpose of God. Our Lord will return literally and visibly, and summon His people with a shout like a trumpet blast. The graves of every dead saint will give up its dead and those still living at that time will be **caught up** with Christ to ever be with Him. That is our blessed hope.

A Plea For Holy Living
1 Peter 1:13-16

You will notice that this section starts with the word **wherefore.** This word points us back to our salvation that Peter has just talked about in the previous verses. Because Christians have such a great salvation we are to be a holy people. Salvation means a change in lifestyle. When the soul is regenerated and the Holy Spirit moves in, it is no longer business as usual.

PREPARATION FOR HOLINESS

Wherefore gird up the loins of your mind, be sober, and hope to the end for the grace that is to be brought unto you at the revelation of Jesus Christ. (1 Peter 1:13) There is a threefold formula here that will prepare us to live a life of holiness.

We Must Be Serious

Peter warns, **gird up the loins of your mind. (1 Peter 1:13a)** What exactly does Peter mean by this command? There was a custom in Bible days of gathering up one's long robes and tying them around the waist. Men did this when they were going to work, run, or walk fast so that they wouldn't trip. Elijah is a good example of a man girding up his loins. **And the hand of the LORD was on Elijah; and he girded up his loins, and ran before Ahab to the entrance of Jezreel. (1 Kings 18:46)** Peter uses this practice as an analogy to illustrate the need to protect our minds. When

Peter said **gird up the loins of your mind,** he was saying don't let your mind trip you up. Many believers trip up and fall because they are not thinking right. **For as he thinketh in his heart, so is he. (Proverbs 23:7a)** Sin has its origin in the thought life. Jesus said, **... From within, out of the heart of men, proceed evil thoughts, adulteries, fornication, murders, thefts, covetousness, wickedness, deceit, lasciviousness, an evil eye, blasphemy, pride, foolishness: All these evil things come from within, and defile the man. (Mark 7:21-23)** It is in the thought life that sin is conceived. When Peter said, **gird up the loins of your mind,** he is telling us to gather up the loose ends of our thought life lest it trip us up. Paul put it this way, **Casting down imaginations, and every high thing that exalteth itself against the knowledge of God, and bringing into captivity every thought to the obedience of Christ. (2 Corinthians 10:5)** This is military language. The term **casting down** speaks of a struggle to defeat the enemy. If you are going to defeat sin there must be an all out war launched against your thought life. You must fight like a soldier, to bring your imaginations under control. Paul says, **bringing into captivity every thought to the obedience of Christ.** The previous verse speaks of **strong holds.** The enemy has set up a stronghold in our mind. Believers still have thoughts and images in their mind from before they were saved. They are things we would like to get rid of, but they are still there. These are enemy strong holds. We are to attack these strong holds and take them captive. Our goal is, **bringing into to captivity every thought.** The idea here is that of taking an enemy soldier as prisoner, and bringing him into obedience.

No longer is he a combatant, he is a prisoner. He is no longer warring against you, he is your prisoner. He no longer controls you, you control him. Rather than sitting around thinking about things that will trip us up, Christians need to recognize that the thought life can be sinful, and therefore, launch an attack and take such thoughts captive. Does your thought life trip you up? Peter said, **gird up the loins of your mind.**

We Must Be Sober

We must **be sober. (1 Peter 1:13b)** We usually think of soberness in connection with abstaining from alcohol, but that is not what Peter is dealing with here. Peter is still talking about our mind. The context here is still the thought life. Just like alcohol will dull your physical senses, impair your judgment, and influence your actions, so will the wrong thoughts. Peter is telling us not to be controlled and intoxicated by wicked thoughts, but to be clear headed and think Scripturally. He uses this same word of being alert in prayer. **But the end of all things is at hand: be ye therefore sober, and watch unto prayer. (1 Peter 4:7)** And of being on the lookout for Satanic attack. **Be sober, be vigilant; because your adversary the devil, as a roaring lion, walketh about, seeking whom he may devour. (1 Peter 5:8)** The idea is that we must be sober minded and clear headed.

We Must Be Searching

We have to keep our heart fixed on the return of Christ. Peter says, **... hope to the end for the grace that is to be brought unto you at the** revelation **of Jesus Christ. (1 Peter**

1:13c) Again Peter mentions the hope of Christ's return. The phrase **to the end** speaks of completion. It points to the end of the Church age when Jesus Christ steps out onto the clouds and sounds the trumpet to call His people home at last. That is our blessed hope. A sober anticipation of the fact that Jesus might come at any moment would certainly clean up our thought lives. The imminent return of Jesus Christ motivates the believer to live a holy life and promotes the purity and separation of the Church from the world.

> **Beloved, now are we the sons of God, and it doth not yet appear what we shall be: but we know that, when he shall appear, we shall be like him; for we shall see him as he is. And every man that hath this hope in him purifieth himself, even as he is pure. (1 John 3:2-3)**

Every man that hath this hope! What hope? The return of Christ—the rapture! The Christian who is expecting the any moment return of Christ will be a committed Christian. The Christian's duty is to live at all times the way he would want his Saviour to find him living at the rapture. Jesus Christ asked the question, **...when the Son of man cometh, shall he find faith on the earth?. (Luke 18:8)** The faithful Christian is living and watching for the return of his Saviour.

> **For the grace of God that bringeth salvation hath appeared to all men, Teaching us that, denying ungodliness and worldly lusts, we should live soberly, righteously, and godly, in this present world; Looking for that blessed hope, and the glorious appearing of the great God and our Saviour Jesus Christ. (Titus 2:11-13)**

There is no greater incentive to living a sanctified life than the imminent return of Christ. Dr. R. A. Torrey said, "*The imminent return of our Lord is the greatest Bible argument for a pure, unselfish, devoted, unworldly, active life of service.*"

PURSUIT OF HOLINESS

As obedient children, not fashioning yourselves according to the former lusts in your ignorance. (1 Peter 1:14) We are to pursue holiness. The Hebrew Christians were instructed to, **Follow peace with all men, and holiness, without which no man shall see the Lord: (Hebrews 12:14)** We are to follow after or go after holiness. We are given two requirements concerning the pursuit of holiness.

There must be Submission

Peter says, **As obedient children.** The first requirement in the pursuit of holiness is obedience. Obedience is the proof of salvation. **And hereby we do know that we know him, if we keep his commandments. (1 John 2:3)** Obedience is the difference between a mere profession and a genuine experience of salvation. Obedience is the voluntary subjection of one's will to the will of another. When the Christian reads the Bible or hears God's Word preached he is to line his life up with the Bible. If one continues to reject the will of God, it is a good sign that he has not been born again. Samuel said to Saul, **For rebellion is as the sin of witchcraft, and stubbornness is as iniquity and idolatry … (1 Samuel 15:23)** Either you obey, which is the proof of your salvation or you disobey which is a sign that you are not saved. Charles Spurgeon said, *"An unchanged life is the sign of an uncleansed heart."* One of the greatest hindrances to the work of Christ is the failure of His people in this matter of obedience. The need of the hour is for God's people to simply submit to the will of God. **Behold, to obey is better than sacrifice, and to hearken than the fat of rams. (1 Samuel 15:22)**

There must be Separation

Peter says, **not fashioning yourselves according to the former lusts in your ignorance.** The word **fashioning** means *"to pattern one's life after."* Before salvation we patterned our life after the world. Peter is saying, now that you are saved, change that. Paul said, **And be not conformed to this world: but be ye transformed by the renewing of your mind…. (Romans 12:2)** The word **conformed** is the same word translated **fashioning** in First Peter. The idea is now that we are saved we do not pattern our life after the world, but after Christ. When one is conformed to the world, he is patterning his actions and life after his former lost lifestyle. It is sad to say, but many professing Christians are still children of worldly lusts rather than children of obedience. Peter calls for a separation from that kind of lifestyle.

There must be Schooling

Peter speaks of their former lifestyle as a life lived **according to … ignorance.** The Christian life is a learning experience. To get saved is to enter into the school of Christ. Jesus said, **learn of me. (Matthew 11:29)** Our first and continuing priority as a Christian is to learn all we can about our Saviour and His ways. The word **ignorant** speaks of lacking information or intelligence concerning a matter. We patterned ourselves according to the world before we were saved because we were ignorant. The lost are described as **Having the understanding darkened, being alienated from the life of God through the ignorance that is in them, because of the blindness of their heart. (Ephesians 4:18)** The lost man lives in ignorance. He is ignorant of God's word and God's will for his life. But a Christian is not ignorant. He has God's Word to inform him and God's Spirit who guide him. One of the first things we learn in the School of Christ is that that we are a new creature and old things are passed away. (2 Corinthians 5:17)

PRIORITY OF HOLINESS

But as he which hath called you is holy, so be ye holy in all manner of conversation. Because it is written, Be ye holy; for I am holy. (1 Peter 1:15-16) The bottom line is clear. A holy God demands a holy people for His name. **For I am the LORD your God: ye shall therefore sanctify yourselves, and ye shall be holy; for I am holy: neither shall ye defile yourselves …. (Leviticus 11:44)** Jesus said, **Be ye therefore perfect, even as your Father which is in heaven is perfect. (Matthew 5:48)** Perfection is God's plan for every believer. Many Christians limit their salvation to a quick prayer and a cheap profession. They have a profession of Christ on their lips, but they have no proof of Christ in their life. However, God takes our holiness seriously. **Having therefore these promises, dearly**

beloved, let us cleanse ourselves from all filthiness of the flesh and spirit, perfecting holiness in the fear of God. (2 Corinthians 7:1) We are to perfect holiness in our lives. The word **perfecting** speaks of *finishing, completing,* or *fulfilling.* It carries the idea of bringing something to its ultimate conclusion. God's people are to be an holy people. In his second letter Peter wrote, **Seeing then that all these things shall be dissolved, what manner of persons ought ye to be in all holy conversation and godliness. (2 Peter 3:11)** God still demands holiness and therefore holiness must be a priority in the life of every believer. **Follow peace with all men, and holiness, without which no man shall see the Lord. (Hebrews 12:14)**

Our Great Redemption
1 Peter 1:18-21

The whole human race is a family of bankrupt beggars. All we ever had, Adam lost to the devil in the garden of Eden. Man was left naked, poor, and miserable and could in no way or by no means pay the price for his salvation. Left to himself, man is helpless and hopeless, lost and sentenced to spend eternity in a Devil's hell. **But God, who is rich in mercy, for his great love wherewith he loved us, Even when we were dead in sins, hath quickened us together with Christ,. (by grace ye are saved;) (Ephesians 2:4-5)** Here Peter speaks of the redemption of lost man.

THE PICTURE OF OUR REDEMPTION

The word **redeemed** is a picturesque word and speaks volumes. It is a word that was used in secular Greek of buying freedom for a slave by making a satisfactory payment. That is what Christ did for the Christian. The sinner himself cannot make a satisfactory payment for his sin. The curse of the law rests heavy upon us all—we were under the bondage of sin.

> **Cursed is every one that continueth not in all things which are written in the book of the law to do them. (Galatians 3:10)**

Oh! How impossible it is for fallen man to obey the law of God. The curse was upon us all for **all have sinned and come short of the glory of God. (Romans 3:23)** The debt of sin must be paid and we being sinners cannot pay the price.

Remember, the payment must be satisfactory. The best that we can do, God cannot accept.

> **But we are all as an unclean thing, and all our righteousnesses are as filthy rags; and we all do fade as a leaf; and our iniquities, like the wind, have taken us away. (Isaiah 64:6)**

Therefore, Jesus Christ purchased redemption for man by paying the price demanded and satisfying the demands of the law. The law demanded the death penalty and Jesus Christ, God's sacrificial Lamb, took the sinner's place and paid that penalty in full.

THE PURITY OF OUR REDEMPTION

Forasmuch as ye know that ye were not redeemed with corruptible things, as silver and gold, from your vain conversation received by tradition from your fathers. (1 Peter 1:18) Our redemption was not purchased with some valuable earthly commodity like silver or gold. We place a dollar value on almost everything. We ask how much does it cost? We value clothes, cars, houses and other possessions in terms of dollars and cents. We consider gold to be the most precious and valuable of metals here, but in Heaven the streets are paved with it. When the end comes and this old world is judged gold and silver will perish with everything else. Gold and silver will be worthless.

Our redemption was not purchased with something that will lose its value and perish someday. Our redemption was purchased with something that will never lose its value—the precious blood of Christ. **For thus saith the LORD, Ye have** sold yourselves for nought; and ye shall be redeemed without money. (Isaiah 52:3)

THE PRICE OF OUR REDEMPTION

But with the precious blood of Christ, as of a lamb without blemish and without spot. (1 Peter 1:19) God invested the Blood of Jesus in our redemption. There is very little preaching on the blood of Christ in our day. The liberals and modernists downplay the blood atonement. They tell us that the shedding of Christ's blood was nothing more than a symbol of His death. However, the Bible is clear when it comes to sin that **without shedding of blood is no remission. (Hebrews 9:22)** Without the shed blood of Jesus Christ, there is no salvation. **In whom we have redemption through his blood, the forgiveness of sins. (Ephesians 1:7a)** Speaking of Christ the Bible says, **And he is the propitiation for our sins: and not for ours only, but also for the sins of the whole world. (1 John 2:2)** The word **propitiation** carries the idea of satisfaction. Relating to salvation God's righteous demands had to be satisfied and we see here that it is Christ who met that demand of sinless perfection and satisfied God.

Paul spoke of our propitiation in his letter to the Romans. **Being justified freely by his grace through the redemption that is in Christ Jesus: Whom God hath set forth to be a propitiation through faith in his blood, to declare his righteousness for the remission of sins that are past, through the forbearance of God. (Romans 3:24-25)** Notice again that our redemption is based upon Christ's propitiation. The New Testament word **propitiation** is the same word that is interpreted **mercy seat** in the Old

Testament. The word **propitiation** takes us back to the Holy of Holies. The Mercy Seat was over the Ark of the Covenant, which enclosed the two tables of the law of God and Aaron's rod that budded. In order to understand more fully what the blood of Christ means to the believer, we will look at some details concerning the Mercy Seat.

First, the Mercy Seat was a ***Meeting Place***. The Mercy Seat was the place where God would meet and commune with the High Priest.

> **And thou shalt put the mercy seat above upon the ark; and in the ark thou shalt put the testimony that I shall give thee. And there I will meet with thee, and I will commune with thee from above the mercy seat, from between the two cherubims which are upon the ark of the testimony, of all things which I will give thee in commandment unto the children of Israel. (Exodus 25:21-22)**

When the Israelites were in the desert after having left Egypt, God gave them instructions to build the Tabernacle. In the Tabernacle the central piece of furniture was the ark. (Exodus 25:10-22) The ark was an oblong chest measuring 45 x 27 x 27 inches. It was made of shittem wood and overlaid inside and out with gold. The lid of the ark, made of solid gold, was called the mercy seat. Here on this lid the atoning blood was applied. God meets man where the blood is applied. There is no other meeting place. Only on the grounds of the precious shed blood of Christ can we have fellowship with God.

Second, the Mercy Seat was a ***Merciful Place***. Leviticus chapter sixteen gives in detail the instructions concerning sacrifice, the blood, and the mercy seat. We learn that on the day of atonement the High Priest would sacrifice a bullock for the sins of Israel. He would then take a basin of the bullock's blood, and enter into the holy of holies to sprinkle the blood on the mercy seat. Dipping his finger into the basin of blood, he sprinkled the mercy seat seven times. (Leviticus 16:14) The blood made it possible for God to show mercy to the nation of Israel. The mercy seat became the place of **propitiation** where God met with the High Priest, accepted the blood as satisfactory payment, and forgave Israel of their sins.

Third, the Mercy Seat was a ***Modeled Place***. Everything about the Tabernacle including the ark and the mercy seat was a model of that which is in Heaven.

> **The Holy Ghost this signifying, that the way into the holiest of all was not yet made manifest, while as the first tabernacle was yet standing: Which was a figure for the time then present, in which were offered both gifts and sacrifices, that could not make him that did the service perfect, as pertaining to the conscience. (Hebrews 9:8-9)**

Paul uses the term **figure** when speaking of the earthly Tabernacle.

> **For Christ is not entered into the holy places made with hands, which are the figures of the true; but into heaven itself, now to appear in the presence of God for us. (Hebrews 9:24)**

A figure is something that is used to represent something else. The Tabernacle on earth was a model or a figure of things in Heaven.

There are many types and symbols in the Tabernacle. We will look at the mercy seat which is clearly a type of the Lord Jesus Christ. **Being justified freely by his grace through the redemption that is in Christ Jesus: Whom God hath set forth to be a propitiation through faith in his blood, to declare his righteousness for the remission of sins that are past, through the forbearance of God. (Romans 3:24-25)** You will remember that the tables of law were inside the ark and covered by the mercy seat. The Holy Spirit has given us the typical meaning of the mercy seat. The same Greek word is used for **mercyseat. (Hebrews 9:5)**, and for **propitiation. (Romans 3:25)** Christ is the One whom God has set forth as the Mercy Seat. Christ, as the Mercy Seat, is the One who has covered the law, and satisfied all of its demands. The law demanded of every man perfect obedience, or death. Jesus Christ covered that demand and became the believer's Mercy Seat. As the High Priest, He entered into Heaven with His own blood satisfying the righteous demands of Almighty God. **Neither by the blood of goats and calves, but by his own blood he entered in once into the holy place, having obtained eternal redemption for us. (Hebrews 9:12)** Jesus was on His way to present the blood as the High Priest in Heaven when He said to Mary, **Touch me not; for I am not yet ascended to my Father: but go to my brethren, and say unto them, I ascend unto my Father, and your Father; and to my God, and your God. (John 20:17)** Notice the words Jesus used here, **my Father, and your Father; and to my God, and your God.** Here He was clearly mediating between God and man—the work of the High Priest. It is only through Jesus Christ that God can meet man, show him mercy, and forgive his sins. **For there is one God, and one mediator between God and men, the man Christ Jesus. (1 Timothy 2:5) Herein is love, not that we loved God, but that he loved us, and sent his Son to be the propitiation for our sins. (1 John 4:10)** No wonder the Bible is so clear that without the shedding of blood there is no remission of sin.

Another detail that needs to be pointed out concerning the blood atonement of Christ is that it was shed for everyone. **And he is the propitiation for our sins: and not for ours only, but also for the sins of the whole world. (1 John 2:2)** The Bible knows nothing of *limited atonement.* Whosoever will may come and partake of the free gift of salvation. **The next day John seeth Jesus coming unto him, and saith, Behold the Lamb of God, which taketh away the sin of the world. (John 1:29)** Praise God it doesn't say, *sins of the elect* or, *sins of the elite* or *the sins of this group* or that group. Oh no! He **taketh away the sin of the world.** John said, **the whole world** Jesus paid the penalty for every sinner who was ever born on earth and everyone that will be born. Surely we understand why Peter called it **precious blood.**

THE PLAN OF OUR REDEMPTION

Who verily was foreordained before the foundation of the world, but was manifest in these last times for you. (1 Peter 1:20) Our redemption was planned by God in eternity. The determination that Christ would pay the price to redeem fallen man was settled by the Godhead **before the foundation of the world.** In Peter's sermon to the Jews on the day of Pentecost he said of Christ, **Him, being delivered**

by the determinate counsel and foreknowledge of God, ye have taken, and by wicked hands have crucified and slain. (Acts 2:23) The atoning work of Christ was not some afterthought or Plan B. God was not taken by surprise when man fell. His fall was foreseen and redemption for whosoever will was planned by the Godhead.

THE PROOF OF OUR REDEMPTION

Who by him do believe in God, that raised him up from the dead, and gave him glory; that your faith and hope might be in God. (1 Peter 1:21) The resurrected Christ is living proof that man's redemption has been purchased and paid for. God **raised Him up from the dead, and gave Him glory.** Many men had died on cruel Roman crosses. But God once and for all proved to the world through the resurrection and exaltation of the Lord Jesus that the death of Christ was distinctly different.

> **Wherefore God also hath highly exalted Him, and given Him a name which is above every name: That at the name of Jesus every knee should bow, of things in heaven, and things in earth, and things under the earth; And that every tongue should confess that Jesus Christ is Lord, to the glory of God the Father. (Philippians 2:9-11)**

Notice Peter said, **that your faith and hope might be in God.** The resurrected Christ builds our faith and hope. Just as surely as God raised Christ from the grave he will raise us who believe on Him. What a death blow the resurrection dealt to Satan. Satan tried throughout the Old Testament to stop the prophecy of Genesis 3:15 from being fulfilled. Even at Christ's birth Satan tried to get Him killed and throughout

His ministry Satan constantly moved against Him. When Christ was pronounced dead Satan thought he had won the war. The death of God's creation was Satan's handiwork. Satan put Adam in the grave. He could claim every grave since that day. But when Jesus stepped out of that grave, Death was Conquered and the Devil was Crushed.

THE PRODUCT OF OUR REDEMPTION

Seeing ye have purified your souls in obeying the truth through the Spirit unto unfeigned love of the brethren, see that ye love one another with a pure heart fervently. (1 Peter 1:22) Peter lists two products that are automatically produced when a person is saved.

First, **<u>Compliance With The Bible</u>**. Obedience to God's word produces purity. Jesus said, **Now ye are clean through the word which I have spoken unto you. (John 15:3) Sanctify them through thy truth: thy word is truth. (John 17:17)** It is impossible to live a holy life apart from the word of God.

> **Wherewithal shall a young man cleanse his way? by taking heed thereto according to thy word. (Psalms 119:9)**

How does one get his life right with God and keep it right? The question is quickly answered, **by taking heed thereto according to thy word. (Psalm 119:9)** You will notice that the answer to David's question is not simply the Word of God, but obedience to the Word. The word **heed** means *to mind; to regard with care; to take notice of; to attend to; to observe.* To cleanse your way you must accept the Bible as the final authority and obey it. It was D. L. Moody who said, *The Bible will keep you from sin; or sin will keep you from* *the Bible.* The Word of God cannot help you unless you obey it. That is what Peter is talking about here. These Christians were holy because they had obeyed the truth. If we are going to live a holy life that will be pleasing to God we must live by the Bible. God's Word is the standard for holy living. **Be ye doers of the word, and not hearers only, deceiving your ownselves. (James 1:22)** The bottom line is obedience.

Second, **<u>Compassion For The Brethren</u>**. Peter continues, **unto unfeigned love of the brethren, see that ye love one another with a pure heart fervently.** Nothing is more important than love in practical Christianity. Our love for one another is a result of Christ's love for us. Jesus said:

> **Greater love hath no man than this, that a man lay down his life for his friends. (John 15:13)**

Jesus Christ put principle into picture. If you want to see true biblical love—look at Christ. Jesus said:

> **This is my commandment, That ye love one another, as I have loved you. (John 15:12)**

The command to love one another was new in the sense that Jesus gave it a new standard. Moses said, **thou shalt love thy neighbour as thyself. (Leviticus 19:18)** The new standard set by Jesus is, **that ye love one another; as I have loved you. (John 13:34)** To love people the way Jesus did, means to love them unconditionally. Love for the brethren is proof of salvation, while hate for others is a good indication that salvation has not taken place.

> **He that saith he is in the light, and hateth his brother, is in darkness even until now. But he that hateth his brother is in darkness, and walketh in darkness, and knoweth not whither he goeth,**

because that darkness hath blinded his eyes. (1 John 2:9 & 11)

A man who claims to be a Christian and hates others is a deceived man. John looks at the Christian's compassion as a test of his conversion. Our compassion for others proves our Christianity. **A new commandment I give unto you, That ye love one another; as I have loved you, that ye also love one another. By this shall all men know that ye are my disciples, if ye have love one to another. (John 13:34-35)** Our love and care of one another gives the lost world a picture of God's love for them.

THE PREACHING OF OUR REDEMPTION

Being born again, not of corruptible seed, but of incorruptible, by the word of God, which liveth and abideth for ever. For all flesh is as grass, and all the glory of man as the flower of grass. The grass withereth, and the flower thereof falleth away: But the word of the Lord endureth for ever. And this is the word which by the gospel is preached unto you. (1 Peter 1:23-25) The new birth is brought about through the agency of the Word of God. The Word of God is the instrument by which the new birth is preached. The word we preach is **incorruptible**. This is the third time that something is listed as **incorruptible** in this chapter. Our eternal inheritance is incorruptible. (1 Peter 1:3,4) God redeemed us by the incorruptible blood of Christ. (1 Peter 1:18,19) And here in verse 23 we have the **incorruptible** word of God. The word incorruptible means *not liable to corruption or decay*. It speaks of that which will never die. Peter spells it out. **The grass withereth, and the flower thereof falleth away: But**

the word of the Lord endureth for ever. God's word is here to stay. Voltaire, the French infidel, said that within thirty years after his death the Bible would pass "*into the limbo of forgotten literature.*" Today the very house in which Voltaire lived belongs to the French Bible Society and is used as a storehouse for Bibles. The very walls that once sheltered the skeptic infidel are now lined with copies of God's Word. **For ever, O LORD, thy word is settled in heaven. (Psalm 119:89)** It is certain the devil hates God's Word. He has tried for centuries to destroy it along with the faith of millions. Many have pronounced its demise, but they're gone and faithful men are still proclaiming the Word of God every day. Jesus said, **Heaven and earth shall pass away: but my words shall not pass away. (Mark 13:31)** The enemies of God can come against it with their blasphemous threatenings, but the Old Book has weathered every storm. Every opponent has been defeated. The Bible has been opened and read at the graves of its infidel enemies. **The grass withereth, the flower fadeth: but the word of our God shall stand for ever. (Isaiah 40:8)**

It's Time To grow Up
1 Peter 2:1-3

Here in the second chapter Peter uses several analogies to communicate the truth of what it means to be a Christian. While chapter one emphasized the importance of being born into the family of God, chapter two stresses the necessity of growing into a mature Christian.

A DISCERNMENT CONCERNING OUR SALVATION

You will notice that Peter starts this passage with the word **wherefore.** He takes us back to the salvation that was produced by the incorruptible word of God in the previous chapter. In other words, what Peter is about to say is based upon what he has just said. The idea is that since God has done a work in our heart, it ought to show up in our life.

A DEPARTURE CONCERNING OUR SIN

Wherefore laying aside all malice, and all guile, and hypocrisies, and envies, and all evil speakings. (1 Peter 2:1) Peter uses the phrase **laying aside.** These words carry the idea of a person stripping off soiled clothing and casting it aside. Next, Peter gives us a list of five things that must be put off if we are to grow and have victory.

1) We must lay aside **all malice.** Webster defines **malice** as "*Extreme enmity of heart, or malevolence; a disposition to injure others without cause, from mere personal gratification or from a spirit of revenge; unprovoked*

malignity or spite." Malice is a driving desire and determination to destroy someone.

2) We must lay aside **all guile.** The word **guile** speaks of craftiness, trickery and dishonesty. The underlying word means *to trick or catch with bait.* This word was a trappers term used to describe the cunning and deceit that is needed to lure an animal into the trap.

3) We must lay aside **hypocrisies.** Hypocrisy is the act of disguising oneself and hiding or operating under a false appearance. Noah Webster defines a hypocrite as *One who feigns to be what he is not; one who has the form of godliness without the power, or who assumes an appearance of piety and virtue, when he is destitute of true religion.* The word hypocrite was originally a theatrical term. It was used in the Greek and Roman theaters to describe an actor. A lot of professing Christians fit the definition. Jesus dealt firmly with the hypocrites in Matthew 23:1-13, who were wicked men pretending to be holy and righteous. They were leading people to hell by just putting on an act of religion.

4) We must lay aside **envies.** Envy is one of the ugliest sins of man. Noah Webster defines envy as, *To feel uneasiness, mortification or discontent, at the sight of superior excellence, reputation or happiness enjoyed by another; to repine at another's prosperity; to fret or grieve one's self at the real or supposed superiority of another, and to hate him on that account.* Envy and jealousy are not quite the same, but they are closely related. Jealousy is fear of losing something that we

already possess. Envy involves a desire to possess something that really belongs to another and to which we have no right. It may be position, promotion, property, privilege, or prestige. This kind of sin is associated with **emulations.** Webster defines emulation as, *The act of attempting to equal or excel in qualities or actions; rivalry; desire of superiority, attended with effort to attain to it.* Envy and emulations are manifested as a constant desire to outrival other people to get the admiration and loyalty of others. **For jealousy is the rage of a man: therefore he will not spare in the day of vengeance. (Proverbs 6:34)** Envy is a sin that is listed as one of the works of the flesh in (Galatians 5:26).

5) We must lay aside **all evil speakings.** Evil speaking is slander, backbiting, angry expressions, tale-bearing and such sins of the tongue. Dr. John R. Rice who said, "*More people sin with the tongue than any other way.*" James had a great deal to say about the tongue. **If any man among you seem to be religious, and bridleth not his tongue, but deceiveth his own heart, this man's religion is vain. (James 1:26)** If a man claims to be a mature Christian but can't keep his own tongue from corrupt communication, he has already identified himself as deceived and his religion is vain. James went on to say, **And the tongue is a fire, a world of iniquity: so is the tongue among our members, that it defileth the whole body, and setteth on fire the course of nature; and it is set on fire of hell. (James 3:6)** A loose and smoldering tongue is not lit with any ordinary fire, it is **set on fire of hell.** The work of the uncontrolled tongue is a product of

hell. Oh! The heartaches that have been caused by angry and bitter Christians who have turned the reigns of their tongues over to hell.

A DESIRE CONCERNING THE SCRIPTURES

As newborn babes, desire the sincere milk of the word, that ye may grow thereby. (1 Peter 2:2) Peter uses the analogy of a newborn baby's hunger for milk to emphasize the believer's need to feed upon the word of God. There are three important thoughts in this verse.

The Passion

Peter says that newborn babies **desire** milk. The word **desire** carries the idea of an *intense craving*. The idea is not that he just wants milk, but that he can't do without it. This intense craving for milk is a sign of life. So, longing for the Word of God is a sure manifestation of spiritual life. People who profess salvation, but have no hunger for the word of God really concern me. Newborn babies come into this world hungry. The first thing they want is milk. A baby is hungry **first** and he is hungry **frequently**. Anyone who has ever had a baby in the house understands this analogy. If you have ever been awakened at 3 a.m. by a crying baby then you understand that nothing except a fresh bottle of warm milk will do. The idea is that just as that baby's life revolves around milk, our lives ought to revolve around the Word of God.

The Purity

Peter calls it **sincere milk.** The word **sincere** means to be *pure and uncontaminated*. A baby's milk must be pure and uncontaminated. If a mother is on certain medicines she can't breast feed. When babies are bottle fed great precautions are taken to sterilize bottles and only fresh milk is used. Why? Because impurities will greatly effect the baby's health. The same is true with the believer. He is to feed upon the unpolluted, uncontaminated, unadulterated word of God. There are a lot of unhealthy Christians out there with foolish and false ideas because they have been feeding on a perverted version rather than the pure version of God's word. God knew folks would try to pervert His word, so He stress the fact that we need the **sincere** word.

The Product

Peter said, **that ye may grow thereby.** Just as a newborn baby needs physical nourishment to grow, the Christian needs the spiritual nourishment of God's word. Jesus said, **Man shall not live by bread alone, but by every word that proceedeth out of the mouth of God. (Matthew 4:4)** Babies do not remain babies. They grow into adults. Just as parents expect their children to grow physically, so God expects His children to grow spiritually. A baby that doesn't grow is a sick baby and a Christian who doesn't grow is a sick Christian.

So many Christians are sick and are not growing because of their neglect of the word of God. David said, **Through thy precepts I get understanding: therefore I hate every false way. (Psalm 119:104)** David knew and despised the false ways because he was familiar with the precepts of God. Jesus said, **Ye do err, not knowing the scriptures. (Matthew 22:29)** The Word of God is food for our spiritual lives. It is the final authority in all matters of faith and practice. The physical man lives by bread, but the spiritual man lives by every word that proceeds from our heavenly Father. No wonder Job said, **I have esteemed the words of his mouth more than my necessary food. (Job 23:12)** Think about the trials that Job was going through! What a lesson! God's Word was more precious to him during his trials than anything else he could imagine. The Bible is the spiritual food by which we grow in grace. Is your spiritual growth stunted? Are you hungry for a good spiritual meal? Then pull up to God's table and let Him feed you with the pure Word of God .

A DELIGHT CONCERNING THE SAVIOUR

If so be ye have tasted that the Lord is gracious. (1 Peter 2:3) What a delight to have tasted of the Lord's grace. Peter alludes to Psalm 34. The background for this Psalm is found in 1st Samuel chapter 21. There we find David fleeing from Saul and taking refuge in the cave of Adullam. It was during these trouble times that David cried, **O taste and see that the LORD is good: blessed is the man that trusteth in him. (Psalms 34:8)** If you will feast upon the word and grow up in the Lord every situation can be one of tasting God's goodness.

Building On The Rock
1 Peter 2:4-10

Peter now uses a new metaphor. He moves on from babes to compares believers to a priesthood serving in the Temple.

A SURE FOUNDATION

To whom coming, as unto a living stone, disallowed indeed of men, but chosen of God, and precious ... Wherefore also it is contained in the scripture, Behold, I lay in Sion a chief corner stone, elect, precious . (1 Peter 2:4, 6) Jesus Christ is presented as the living stone upon which the church is built. Peter also makes note that this Stone was **disallowed indeed of men.** The word **disallowed** means to be *"disapproved of and rejected."* He was **chosen of God, and precious,** but man rejected Him. **He came unto his own, and his own received him not. (John 1:11)** How tragic that prideful and fallen man rejects God's Christ.

The Stone is a familiar metaphor of Christ throughout Scripture. In this passage He is the Living Stone. (4) the Cornerstone. (6) the Headstone. (7) and the Stone of stumbling. (8) The Psalmist prophesied, **The stone which the builders refused is become the head stone of the corner. (Psalms 118:22)** Christ applied these words to His own rejection. (Matthew 21:42) Peter and John used this same reference when they were being tried by the Sanhedrin. (Acts 4:11) Paul draws from the analogy of the

Stone. (Romans 9:32-33) Isaiah prophesied, **Therefore thus saith the Lord GOD, Behold, I lay in Zion for a foundation a stone, a tried stone, a precious corner stone, a sure foundation: he that believeth shall not make haste. (Isaiah 28:16)** Whenever you think of a foundation, you think of something that is solid, strong and stable. If your foundation isn't right, your house will not be secure.

> **If the foundations be destroyed, what can the righteous do? (Psalms 11:3)**

Jesus said,

> **Therefore whosoever heareth these sayings of mine, and doeth them, I will liken him unto a wise man, which built his house upon a rock: And the rain descended, and the floods came, and the winds blew, and beat upon that house; and it fell not: for it was founded upon a rock. (Matthew 7:24-25)**

Jesus Christ is the foundation Stone of God's redemption. **For other foundation can no man lay than that is laid, which is Jesus Christ. (1 Corinthians 3:11)** Everything rests upon Christ. He is the solid, strong and stable foundation of our salvation. A structure will not last unless it is built upon a solid foundation. Here we learn that the household of God is built upon a solid and sure foundation. Paul said,

> **According to the grace of God which is given unto me, as a wise masterbuilder, I have laid the foundation, and another buildeth thereon. But let every man take heed how he buildeth thereupon.**

> For other foundation can no man lay than that is laid, which is Jesus Christ. (1 Corinthians 3:10-11)

My hope is built on nothing less than Jesus blood and righteousness.

A SPIRITUAL FAMILY

Ye also, as lively stones, are built up a spiritual house, an holy priesthood, to offer up spiritual sacrifices, acceptable to God by Jesus Christ ... But ye are a chosen generation, a royal priesthood, an holy nation, a peculiar people; that ye should shew forth the praises of him who hath called you out of darkness into his marvellous light. (1 Peter 2:5, 9) The picture here is that of the Old Testament Temple. In the Old Testament, God's temple was a temporal and material house. (Luke 21:5; John 2:20) However, in the New Testament, believers **are built up a spiritual house.** Paul wrote to the Ephesians:

> **Now therefore ye are no more strangers and foreigners, but fellowcitizens with the saints, and of the household of God; And are built upon the foundation of the apostles and prophets, Jesus Christ himself being the chief corner stone; In whom all the building fitly framed together groweth unto an holy temple in the Lord: In whom ye also are builded together for an habitation of God through the Spirit. (Ephesians 2:19-22)**

The analogy of the house speaks volumes.

First, our *__Family__*. **Now therefore ye are no more strangers and foreigners, but fellowcitizens with the saints, and of the household of God. (Ephesians 2:19)** We

are no more strangers and foreigners. We are no longer Despised, Distant, and Divided—no longer on the outside looking in. We have been Delivered! The child of God is not merely saved. Salvation alone is wonderful and far more than we deserve. But on top of that, we have been adopted into the family of God. Adoption is an important New Testament doctrine.

> **But when the fulness of the time was come, God sent forth his Son, made of a woman, made under the law, To redeem them that were under the law, that we might receive the adoption of sons. (Galatians 4:4-5)**

The adoption of the child of God is a powerful and life changing truth. When we adopt a child the best we can do is give him our name and try to raise and train him for the Lord. Though in every aspect we treat him like a son and love him like our own, we still cannot impart unto him our nature. However, it is quite different with God. God doesn't simply fill out the papers and take us on for support. He literally becomes our Father and we his children. **But as many as received him, to them gave he power to become the sons of God, even to them that believe on his name. (John 1:12)** As God's children we are not just placed into the family, we literally become **partakers of the divine nature. (2 Peter 1:4)**

Second, our *Framing.* **In whom all the building fitly framed together groweth unto an holy temple in the Lord: In whom ye also are builded together for an habitation of God through the Spirit. (Ephesians 2:21-22)** This verse speaks of the unity of the body. We are to be **fitly framed**

together. This is a builder's term that carries the idea of *the careful joining of every part of a piece of furniture or building.* Each piece of wood has to be precisely cut and then many times trimmed and sanded to get the right fit and finish. This is the picture that God uses of us. Everyone who comes to Christ is taken by God and **fitly framed** into the proper place in the building.

Third, our **Function**. Peter says of believers, **But ye are a chosen generation, a royal priesthood, an holy nation, a peculiar people; that ye should shew forth the praises of him who hath called you out of darkness into his marvellous light. (1 Peter 2:9)** What a privilege to live on the New Testament side of the cross. In the Old Testament only the high priest could enter into the presence of God, and then, only once a year. As New Testament believers we have access to God's presence at any time. We can without the aid of a priest go, **boldly unto the throne of grace, that we may obtain mercy, and find grace in the time of need. (Hebrews 4:16)** We have **boldness to enter into the holiest by the blood of Jesus. (Hebrews 10:19)** The Believer does not need a priest or a church to intercede on his behalf to God. The believer can boldly, by the fact of being washed in the blood of Christ, instantly be in contact with God by simple prayer. He can further bring his petitions or requests for forgiveness of sins directly to God himself.

A SAD FAILURE

Peter says, **but unto them which be disobedient, the stone which the builders disallowed, the same is made the head of the corner, And a stone of stumbling, and a rock**

of offence, even to them which stumble at the word, being disobedient: whereunto also they were appointed. (1 Peter 2:7-8) In spite of the wonderful truth that Jesus Christ is available to everyone, many refuse Him as their Savior. They are unbelieving and disobedient. God made Him the cornerstone, but they reject Him. They build their lives on unbelief as they worship the gods of pleasure and prosperity. Such people continually stumble and fall over who Jesus Christ is. To their own destruction, they refuse to accept Him and acknowledge Him as the One upon whom they are to build.

Christian Living In A Wicked World
1 Peter 2:11-12

God's people are in the world, but not of the world. Jesus said, **I have chosen you out of the world. (John 15:19)** Peter stress the point that we are to be different.

WE ARE TRAVELERS

Dearly beloved, I beseech you as strangers and pilgrims.... (1 Peter 2:11a) It is important for us to remember that we are not settlers in this world, we are strangers. Peter uses two words here to stress the fact that we are not part of this world system. The word **stranger** carries the idea of "*a sojourner or a temporary resident.*" The word **pilgrim** speaks of a "*foreigner traveling through a strange land.*" These are very descriptive terms of what every believer is. We are foreigners to this world. God's people need to grasp this truth. This world is not our home we are mere strangers to here. By way of the new birth we are creatures of another world.

WE WILL HAVE TROUBLE

We are to **abstain from fleshly lusts, which war against the soul. (1 Peter 2:11b)** Peter reminds us that our flesh wars against or soul. This is the war that rages within the very being of every Christian. Before salvation, we had only one nature. Now that we are saved, we still have that same old nature, but through the new birth we have received a new nature. It is a spiritual nature, what the Bible calls a **divine nature. (2 Peter 1:4)** The two natures of the believer are at war with one another and the Christian's heart is the battleground. The new nature wants to do that which pleases God, while the old nature resists submitting to the Spirit and doing those things which please God. The old depraved nature and the new Divine power of God are at war for the believer's will.

Paul put it this way. **For the flesh lusteth against the Spirit, and the Spirit against the flesh: and these are contrary the one to the other: so that ye cannot do the things that ye would. (Galatians 5:17)** The word **lusteth** speaks of a *"strong desire."* Paul states that the Spirit and the flesh lust **against** each other, meaning they have opposite desires for us. The flesh wants us to succumb to sin while the Spirit wants us to live for Christ. Paul goes on to say that **these are contrary the one to the other.** The word **contrary** means to *"oppose or confront."* Here is the reason for the conflict that Christians have in their life as they struggle to put off the old and put on the new. The flesh dictates that we be one way and the Spirit immediately steps up and opposes the sinful nature and demands that we walk in the Spirit. The same word used here for **contrary** is translated **adversaries** in Luke 13:17 and 1 Corinthians 16:9. An adversary is an enemy or a foe. The flesh and the Spirit are adversaries—they are enemies one of another. They are not going to compromise and will never be at peace. The battle rages as these two adversaries fight to gain ground in the Christian's life.

We must make a decision as to which one of these natures we are going to side with. Our marching orders are from God. Paul said, **That ye put off concerning the former conversation the old man, which is corrupt according to the deceitful lusts; And be renewed in the spirit of your mind; And that ye put on the new man, which after God is** created in righteousness and true holiness. **(Ephesians 4:22-24)** Paul also commanded the Colossian believers to **put off all these; anger, wrath, malice, blasphemy, filthy communication out of your mouth. Lie not one to another, seeing that ye have put off the old man with his deeds; And have put on the new man, which is renewed in knowledge after the image of him that created him. (Colossians 3:8-10)** In the terminology of putting off and putting on Paul compared the Christian life to stripping off the filthy clothes of a sinful past and putting on the white robes of Christ's righteousness. Such is a radical change for the sinful nature to encounter and accept. Jesus said, **That which is born of the flesh is flesh; and that which is born of the Spirit is spirit. (John 3:6)** With two opposing natures abiding in one body there is a constant war going on. That which is born of the flesh is flesh and will always be flesh while we are in this body and therefore, goes in direction of depravity. However, that which is born of the Spirit is spirit and desires to go in the opposite direction of the flesh. Which side are you on?

This I say then, Walk in the Spirit, and ye shall not fulfil the lust of the flesh. (Galatians 5:16) Here we have the clear command of God to **walk in the Spirit.** Jesus gave us the Holy Spirit to empower us to walk for and serve Him. **I send the promise of my Father upon you: but tarry ye in the city of Jerusalem, until ye be endued with power from on high. (Luke 24:49)** It is the Spirit of God that furnishes the power to live the Christian life. **Not by might, nor by power, but by my spirit, saith the LORD of hosts. (Zechariah 4:6)** Jesus said earlier, **It is the spirit that quickeneth; the flesh profiteth nothing.... (John 6:63)**

You say Preacher, How do I **abstain from fleshly lusts, which war against the soul.** Do as the Scripture commands, **walk in the Spirit.** Obeying that command would settle the matter of walking in the flesh vs. walking in the Spirit. The text is clear! If we do walk in the Spirit we will not **fulfil the lust of the flesh.** We by our will and choice decide the course of conduct we will take. You can decide right now which force will rule in your life. Herein lies the means of victory! **WALK IN THE SPIRIT.** We will have trouble in this world, but we can also have victory.

WE MUST HAVE A TESTIMONY

Having your conversation honest among the Gentiles: that, whereas they speak against you as evildoers, they may by your good works, which they shall behold, glorify God in the day of visitation. (1 Peter 2:12) The word **conversation** carries the idea of *"behavior or conduct."* There are two kinds of conversation. *First*, there is that which we say with our lips. *Secondly*, there it that which we say with our life. Peter is not speaking of our talk, but our walk—our manner of life. He is talking about how we live from day to day.

Peter says that our way of life must be **honest among the Gentiles.** The phrase **among the Gentiles** speaks of the unsaved world around us. The word **honest** demands our attention. The word means *good, valuable and virtuous.* It carries the idea of *beautiful.* We must be careful with our testimony. The great Scottish preacher Alexander Maclaren wrote:

> "The world takes its notions of God, most of all, from the people who say that they belong to God's family. They read us a great deal more than they

read the Bible. They see us; they only hear about Jesus Christ."

What an awesome responsibility we have to live a straight life in a crooked world.

Peter goes on to say, **whereas they speak against you as evildoers.** One thing is for certain. They will speak evil against us. If there is one thing the world hates, it is a Christian who walks upright and in the light. In his book, The Secret of Christian Joy, Vance Havner said:

> Let it not be forgotten that a twice-born and Spirit-filled Christian is always a contradiction to this old world. He crosses it at every point. From the day that he is born again until he passes on to be with the Lord, he pulls against the current of a world forever going the other way. The real firebrand is distressing to the devil, and when a wide-awake believer comes along, taking the Gospel seriously, we can expect sinister maneuvering for his downfall.

Jesus said, **And this is the condemnation, that light is come into the world, and men loved darkness rather than light, because their deeds were evil. For every one that doeth evil hateth the light, neither cometh to the light, lest his deeds should be reproved. But he that doeth truth cometh to the light, that his deeds may be made manifest, that they are wrought in God. (John 3:19-21)** Jesus explains the problem here. Men love darkness because it hides their wicked deeds and they hate light because it exposes their wickedness. Where are you walking? Your lifestyle reflects your heart. You cannot hide. **For ye were sometimes darkness, but now are ye light in the Lord: walk as children of light. (Ephesians 5:8)**

Now Peter says, **they may by your good works, which they shall behold, glorify God in the day of visitation.** The idea here is that we are to walk in such a manner that our good works will prove them wrong. Robert Leighton in his classic commentary wrote:

> "When a Christian walks irreprovably, his enemies have no where to fasten their teeth on him, but are forced to gnaw their own malignant tongues. As it secures the godly, thus to stop the lying mouths of foolish men, so it is as painful to them to be thus stopped, as muzzling is to beasts, and it punishes their malice. And this is a wise Christian's way, instead of impatiently fretting at the mistakes or wilful miscensures of men, to keep still on his calm temper of mind, and upright course of life, and silent innocence; this, as a rock, breaks the waves into foam that roar about it."

Jesus said, **Let your light so shine before men, that they may see your good works, and glorify your Father which is in heaven. (Matthew 5:16)** This is a principle that is found throughout the New Testament. (1 Corinthians 10:32; Colossians 4:5; 1 Thessalonians 4:12; 1 Timothy 3:7; 5:14; 6:1; Titus 2:5-10).

Christian Citizenship
1 Peter 2:13-17

In this section we are reminded of our obligation to be submissive to governmental authority. This was no doubt a hard lesson for these believers to swallow. Submission is not always easy. Depraved and prideful man has a hard time with submission. We must remember that the recipients of this letter were being relentlessly persecuted by the government. They were forced to flee from their homes, leaving nearly everything behind. They had to abandon their family, clothes, homes and jobs. These were trying and difficult times for God's people.

THE ADMONITION TO SUBMISSION

Peter commands, **submit yourselves. (1 Peter 2:13a)** The word **submit** is a military term that means to *line up in rank.* The idea is *lining up in formation under the commander.* Every believer has an obligation to be not only a faithful Christian, but a faithful citizen. Peter has reminded us that we are **strangers and pilgrims. (1 Peter 2:11a),** in this world. So far as this world goes we are pilgrims passing through. Our citizenship is in Heaven.

> **For our conversation is in heaven; from whence also we look for the Saviour, the Lord Jesus Christ. (Philippians 3:20)**

However, we must remember that Heavenly citizenship does not relieve us from earthly responsibilities. In order to

First Peter

be a good Christian, we must be a good citizen and that means submission to authority.

THE ADVANCEMENT OF SUBMISSION

We are to be submissive **for the Lord's sake. (1 Peter 2:13b)** Christianity is not about us, it is all about the Lord Jesus Christ. Peter reminds us that we submit for **the Lord's sake.** This was Paul's attitude when wrongfully imprisoned. Paul used his imprisonment **for the Lord's sake.** Paul recognized the Bible mandate of respecting and honoring those in authority. **But I would ye should understand, brethren, that the things which happened unto me have fallen out rather unto the furtherance of the gospel; So that my bonds in Christ are manifest in all the palace, and in all other places. (Philippians 1:12-13)** In the next chapter Paul wrote, **Do all things without murmurings and disputings: That ye may be blameless and harmless, the sons of God, without rebuke, in the midst of a crooked and perverse nation, among whom ye shine as lights in the world. (Philippians 2:14-15)** When Christians do right and submit to authority it honors the Lord and advances His cause.

THE AREA OF SUBMISSION

We are to submit, **to every ordinance of man for the Lord's sake: whether it be to the king, as supreme; Or unto governors, as unto them that are sent by him for the punishment of evildoers, and for the praise of them that do well. (1 Peter 2:13c-14)** Here is the bottom line. Believers are to respect and obey the law of the land. You will notice that God didn't ask our opinion. He simply says, **submit**

yourselves to every ordinance. Let us keep in mind that these authorities are put in place by God. Paul wrote to the Christians in the Church at Rome urging them to submit obediently and willingly to the authorities. **Let every soul be subject unto the higher powers. For there is no power but of God: the powers that be are ordained of God. (Romans 13:1)** A few verses later Paul explained:

> **For he is the minister of God to thee for good. But if thou do that which is evil, be afraid; for he beareth not the sword in vain: for he is the minister of God, a revenger to execute wrath upon him that doeth evil. Wherefore ye must needs be subject, not only for wrath, but also for conscience sake. (Romans 13:4-5)**

Remember when the Lord was on this earth He paid due respect and obeyed the law of the land. Think about it. He possessed all authority and power and not once did He resist or disobey the law. When His taxes were due, He sent Peter down to the sea to catch a fish. His instructions were:

> **Take up the fish that first cometh up; and when thou hast opened his mouth, thou shalt find a piece of money: that take, and give unto them for Me and thee. (Matthew 17:27)**

On another occasion, He commanded,

> **Render therefore unto Caesar the things which are Caesar's; and unto God the things that are God's. (Matthew 22:21)**

The government is put in place by God's providence.

> **For promotion cometh neither from the east, nor from the west, nor from the south. But God is the**

judge: he putteth down one, and setteth up another. (Psalms 75:6-7)

We are to obey the laws of the land. This is one of those areas of Christian living that calls for balance. We have to be extremely careful here. But there are limits to the degree to which we may go in submitting to government. If Government opposes the Word of God and prohibits our freedom of worship, our carrying out the great commission, etc., the Christian is not obligated to consent to such a law. You will remember back in the book of Acts, Peter and the apostles being taken before the high priest and the council. The powers that be asked, **Did not we straitly command you that ye should not teach in this name? and, behold, ye have filled Jerusalem with your doctrine…. (Acts 5:28)** These men were commanded by the authorities to stop preaching the gospel of Christ and they refused to obey. The reason is clear. **Then Peter and the other apostles answered and said, We ought to obey God rather than men. (Acts 5:29)** Obedience to Christ always supersedes our allegiance to others.

THE ACHIEVEMENT OF SUBMISSION

For so is the will of God, that with well doing ye may put to silence the ignorance of foolish men. (1 Peter 2:15) Remember, as believer's we exist in two realms—we are part of two worlds. While we are citizens of Heaven, we are serving on earth as ambassadors. **Now then we are ambassadors for Christ…. (2 Corinthians 5:20)** An ambassador is one who represents his country in a foreign land. As citizens of Heaven may we realize that this world is not our home and God help us to live in this strange land as ambassadors representing our Lord Jesus Christ. There are a lot of foolish and ignorant men who bring up one objection after another about our Christianity, but nothing silences their foolishness like the godliness of a sold out Christian. Their foolishness can easily be silenced by our godly testimony.

THE ATTITUDE OF SUBMISSION

As free, and not using your liberty for a cloke of maliciousness, but as the servants of God. (1 Peter 2:16) Here is where many fail. Anytime that liberty is placed above the law the consequences will be disastrous. The argument is that our liberty in Christ does not exclude us from the responsibility of obeying the law of the land. We live in a self-centered, do your own thing society. Ours is a no restraint lawless society. Authority is constantly being challenged as modern libertines pursue the desires of the flesh. The word **cloke** speaks of a covering. The idea is that we are not to use our liberty in Christ as a covering to avoid man's law. Paul sounded the same warning (Galatians 5:13).

THE APPLICATION OF SUBMISSION

Honour all men. Love the brotherhood. Fear God. Honour the king. (1 Peter 2:17) Peter summarizes this passage by giving us four areas of practical application.

First, we are to **Honour all men.** We are to give honor to all men no matter who they are, where they came from or what they stand for.

Second, we are to **Love the brotherhood.** This is interesting! That the Holy Spirit decided to remind us of our duty to one another concerning Christian love. The greatest demonstrations of genuine Christianity is our love for one another. **Beloved, let us love one another: for love is of God; and every one that loveth is born of God, and knoweth God. He that loveth not knoweth not God; for God is love. (1 John 4:7-8)** Our compassion for others, especially for the brethren, is the greatest proof of our salvation. **A new commandment I give unto you, That ye love one another; as I have loved you, that ye also love one another. By this shall all men know that ye are my disciples, if ye have love one to another. (John 13:34-35)** Our love and care of one another gives the lost world a picture of God's love for them.

Third, we are to **Fear God.** The fact that we have a duty to fear God is a major teaching throughout the Word of God. (Deuteronomy 13:4; Psalm 111:10; Proverbs 9:10; Ecclesiastes 12:13; Hebrews 12:28) The world needs to see the fear of God in believers. If we obey this command to fear God we will have no problem obeying the rest of the passage.

Fourth, we are to **Honour the king.** Many times we will disagree with someone in authority, but we must still show honor for them. Paul wrote, **Render therefore to all their dues: tribute to whom tribute is due; custom to whom custom; fear to whom fear; honour to whom honour. (Romans 13:7)** When believers obey the principles of this passage, our obedience gives credibility to our faith and brings glory to God.

When Life Isn't Fair
1 Peter 2:18-25

Peter now instructs us on how to submit even when life just isn't fair. Here is one of the most heard cries of the day. That's not fair. The bottom line is that life is not always going to be fair. **Yet man is born unto trouble, as the sparks fly upward. (Job 5:7)** Man will have trouble. In this section Peter points out that life on this earth wasn't fair for Christ either. He didn't quit, He didn't retaliate, He didn't complain. Instead He **for the joy that was set before him endured the cross, despising the shame, and is set down at the right hand of the throne of God. (Hebrews 12:2)** That is our example.

THE EXTREME OF SLAVERY

Servants, be subject to your masters with all fear; not only to the good and gentle, but also to the froward. (1 Peter 2:18) The workforce in the Roman world was made up of slaves. During the writing of 1 Peter there were between sixty and eighty million slaves in Rome. These slaves were household servants who lived with their masters and served in the home. Many of these slaves were doctors, teachers, musicians and even stewards over their Master's estate. Many of them were well loved and treated as members of the family. However, the Romans looked upon a slave as a possession, rather than a person. These slaves were not free to do their own thing. They were forever to be slaves and they had no legal recourse. These slaves made up a significant number of the early church members.

First Peter

Under inspiration of the Holy Spirit, Peter commands **Servants, be subject to your masters.** Many thought that their conversion would free them from slavery. Not so! The word **subject** means *to be subordinate; to obey, to be under obedience.* This is a principle that is well established in the Bible.

> **Let every man abide in the same calling wherein he was called. Art thou called being a servant? care not for it: but if thou mayest be made free, use it rather. For he that is called in the Lord, being a servant, is the Lord's freeman: likewise also he that is called, being free, is Christ's servant. Ye are bought with a price; be not ye the servants of men. Brethren, let every man, wherein he is called, therein abide with God. (1 Corinthians 7:20-24)**

> **Let as many servants as are under the yoke count their own masters worthy of all honour, that the name of God and his doctrine be not blasphemed. And they that have believing masters, let them not despise them, because they are brethren; but rather do them service, because they are faithful and beloved, partakers of the benefit. These things teach and exhort. (1 Timothy 6:1-2)**

> **Exhort servants to be obedient unto their own masters, and to please them well in all things; not answering again; Not purloining, but shewing all good fidelity; that they may adorn the doctrine of God our Saviour in all things. (Titus 2:9-10)**

Many of these saved slaves were working in the homes of pagan Masters, but they were to submit to the authority they were under. The Bible says, **rebellion is as the sin of**

witchcraft. (1 Samuel 15:23) God never honors rebellion, He does honor our obedience to authority.

And they were to submit **with all fear.** The phrase with all fear does not mean in fear of the employers wrath. The word **fear** carries the idea of "*fear with reverence* "and is referring to the fear of God. Their attitude was to be one of fear or reverence for God. This was their motivation for submissive service. This passage can easily be applied to employer/employee relationship.

Here comes the hard one. Peter says, **not only to the good and gentle, but also to the froward.** How many times have you heard this used for an excuse? "*Well, I would submit if he wasn't such a jerk."* The **good and gentle** are a lot easier to submit to than the **froward.** However, the servant/employee is to submit whether or not the boss is a jerk. It is interesting that the word **froward** comes from "*skoliois"* and speaks of that which is "*curved or crooked."* It is the word from which we get the medical term scoliosis which describes a curvature of the spinal column. Some of your bosses are going to have attitudes and even do things you don't agree with, but as a servant/employee you are to submit to their authority with all fear.

> **Servants, be obedient to them that are your masters according to the flesh, with fear and trembling, in singleness of your heart, as unto Christ; Not with eyeservice, as menpleasers; but as the servants of Christ, doing the will of God from the heart; With good will doing service, as to the Lord, and not to men: Knowing that whatsoever good thing any man doeth, the same shall he receive of the Lord, whether he be bond or free. And, ye masters, do the same things unto them, forbearing threatening:**

knowing that your Master also is in heaven; neither is there respect of persons with him. (Ephesians 6:5-9)

The masters referred to in this verse were crooked and dishonest. Many were unfair in the way they treated the servant\employees who were under them. However Peter says, be subject to them. The issue here is not the boss. It is not poor little old me. The issue is that we are in full-time Christian service and we are to serve as unto Him. We represent Jesus Christ at our place of employment. The idea is that in the workplace, employees are to submit to employers as if they were serving Christ Himself.

THE EXHORTATION TO SUBMIT

For this is thankworthy, if a man for conscience toward God endure grief, suffering wrongfully. For what glory is it, if, when ye be buffeted for your faults, ye shall take it patiently? but if, when ye do well, and suffer for it, ye take it patiently, this is acceptable with God. (1 Peter 2:19-20) It is one thing to be punished when we deserve it. But is quite another to suffer when we don't deserve it. Peter presses home the fact that our motive in being good servants\employees is to please God. **For this is thankworthy.** This is a powerful thought and one that will help the Christian survive the workplace. The word **thankworthy** is the same word translated **grace** when speaking of the grace of God. **For by grace are ye saved…. (Ephesians 2:8)** God's grace is unmerited favor to man. When we deserved judgment and death God showed us grace. The idea here is simple. The boss may not deserve our obedience, but we are to graciously submit nevertheless. We graciously bestow upon him that which he does not deserve because our obedience pleases God.

THE EXAMPLE OF OUR SAVIOUR

When life isn't fair we can look to Jesus who … **suffered for us, leaving us an example, that ye should follow his steps: (1 Peter 2:21)** Jesus Christ is the believer's great example for life and living.

He is the Standard For Our Service

For even hereunto were ye called: because Christ also suffered for us, leaving us an example, that ye should follow his steps: Who did no sin, neither was guile found in his mouth: Who, when he was reviled, reviled not again; when he suffered, he threatened not; but committed himself to him that judgeth righteously. (1 Peter 2:21-23) Notice the phrase, **leaving us an example**. If we want to know how to respond to injustice just look at the way Jesus responded to it. Jesus suffered as no man before or after Him has ever suffered. He suffered not for His own sin for He was sinless. He suffered for our sin. Our Lord Jesus was beaten, stripped of His clothes and scourged by brutal Roman soldiers. After all of the ridicule, the beatings, all of the injustice, the soldiers led Christ away, **And when they were come unto a place called Golgotha, that is to say, a place of a skull … And they crucified him … (Matthew 27:33, 35a)** Golgotha was the place of execution. It was a place where criminals who were no longer considered fit to live among mankind and were no longer worthy of life were executed for their crime. Roman Crucifixion was one of the most barbaric and agonizing punishments known to fallen man. The victim suffered agonizing pain for hours and sometimes for days before death would finally come.

Only this time it was the Lord Jesus Christ, who had come down from Heaven and who had sought only to save man, who was to be executed. There was no criminal on this cross that day—this was the God of glory who had come to save lost man. He was perfect and sinless. He is the One **Who did no sin, neither was guile found in his mouth. (1 Peter 2:22)** His precious hands which had been devoted only to doing good, were nailed to the cross. His feet which had often been tired and sore from the long journeys which He had made through the dusty streets as He carried the good news of salvation to a lost and dying world, were placed upon the cross and pierced with nails. What an injustice, and how did He respond? **Who, when he was reviled, reviled not again; when he suffered, he threatened not.... (1 Peter 2:23a)** He never opened His mouth. He is God! He could have stopped the whole thing. What's more He could have called upon the Angels to deliver Him. **Thinkest thou that I cannot now pray to my Father, and he shall presently give me more than twelve legions of angels? (Matthew 26:53)** A Roman legion was six thousand. Jesus Christ could have called to His aid seventy-two thousand angels. What a Saviour! When He had every right to protest and by His mighty power set everything straight, He never opened His mouth. Isaiah say, **He was oppressed, and he was afflicted, yet he opened not his mouth: he is brought as a lamb to the slaughter, and as a sheep before her shearers is dumb, so he openeth not his mouth. (Isaiah 53:7)** Jesus Christ, the Lamb of God, like a sheep lead to the slaughter quietly and humbly went with them. The Bible says, **but committed himself to him that judgeth righteously. (1 Peter 2:23b)** Now why didn't Jesus revile and threaten them? Because He had already committed the whole situation to God the Father. Jesus Christ's commitment to the will of God and His confidence that God would deal with the injustice was enough. That is the Example we are to follow.

He is the Sacrifice For Our Sins

Who his own self bare our sins in his own body on the tree, that we, being dead to sins, should live unto righteousness: by whose stripes ye were healed. (1 Peter 2:24) Not only did He suffer unjustly, He died unjustly. Just try to imagine Jesus Christ, the perfect and holy, separated from and forsaken of God. **And about the ninth hour Jesus cried with a loud voice, saying, Eli, Eli, lama sabachthani? that is to say, My God, my God, why hast thou forsaken me?. (Matthew 27:46)** Upon Christ Jesus was laid all of the world's sin and therefore, all the Divine wrath of the Holy and Almighty God of Heaven. He was led as a Lamb to the slaughter and it was God Almighty Who led Him there. The day had come that Jesus would be made sin for us. **For he hath made him to be sin for us, who knew no sin; that we might be made the righteousness of God in him. (2 Corinthians 5:21)** Jesus Christ was sinless, but He died forsaken of God because He was bearing the sins of the world. In agony of soul He cries out to His Father **why hast thou forsaken me?** Our dear Lord was dying alone and forsaken of God because He had our sin upon Him. For the first time in eternity, Jesus Christ the eternal Son of God was separated from the Father and it was our sin that separated them.

He is the Shepherd Of Our Souls

For ye were as sheep going astray; but are now returned unto the Shepherd and Bishop of your souls. (1 Peter 2:25) After all of the injustice He experienced, He becomes **Shepherd and Bishop of your souls.** Both of these terms refer to One who protects and provides for someone. With great care, concern, and compassion for us Jesus became our Shepherd. Just think about the condition we were in when Christ saved us. We were lost and headed for Hell. We had no hope apart from Christ. But He saw us one day scattered abroad, as sheep having no shepherd and he was moved with compassion upon us and He saved us. If He had focused on the injustice and called those seventy-two thousand angels to His aid, He would never have been our Saviour. And if we focus on the injustices that come our way, we will fail the cause of Christ.

The Wife Who Wins Her Husband
1 Peter 3:1-6

Peter continues his teaching on submission. He has dealt with submission to government, submission to the boss and in this passage we come to the third category—wives are to submit to their husbands.

HER BEHAVIOR IS INDISPENSABLE

Likewise, ye wives, be in subjection to your own husbands; that, if any obey not the word, they also may without the word be won by the conversation of the wives; While they behold your chaste conversation coupled with fear. (1 Peter 3:1-2) This is an important passage for saved women who want to see their unsaved husbands come to Christ. Her behavior will either be a help or a hindrance. The word **likewise** means *"after the same manner; in a similar way."* When Peter commanded that we be submissive to the government, he said, **Submit yourselves to every ordinance of man for the Lord's sake... (1 Peter 2:13)** Then Peter commanded servants to be submissive to masters. **Servants be subject to your masters with all fear; not only to the good and gentle, but also to the froward. (1 Peter 2:18)** Notice the phrases, **for the Lord's sake,** (13) and **with all fear; not only to the good and gentle, but also to the froward. (18)** Now Peter says to wives, *"In a similar way, be submissive to your husbands."* The wife is to submit to her husband **for the Lord's sake.** She is to further submit to him whether he is a gentleman or a jerk. She is not to decide when she submits, but her way of life should be one of submission to her husband. This isn't a popular message in our *do your own thing* women's liberation society. Contrary to the opinion of the day, for a woman to submit to her husband is not demeaning. It in no way implies that the woman is inferior to the man.

> **There is neither Jew nor Greek, there is neither bond nor free, there is neither male nor female: for ye are all one in Christ Jesus. (Galatians 3:28)**

It is not an issue of worth, but of order. Our God is a God of order—not chaos. For there to be order there must be submission. Someone has to lead and someone has to follow. Just as government and business require order, so does the home. God has given the responsibility for leadership in the home to the husband.

Likewise indicates that the wife is to submit to her husband just like people submit to their government and like employees submit to their employer. A person who submits is not weak but strong. Our self-centered and self-serving society has missed this truth. Just like the government cannot operate properly without the citizens submission and the business cannot operate effectively without the employees submitting to their bosses, neither can the home be a place of peace and harmony without the wife submitting to her husband.

Peter says, **that, if any obey not the word, they also may without the word be won by the conversation of the wives; While they behold your chaste conversation coupled with fear. (1 Peter 3:1b-2)** A wife's submission is indispensable, not only because it is in obedience to the Lord, but also because it can lead to her lost husband's salvation. There are a lot of saved women who have the whole Church praying for her husband's salvation, but with her actions at home she is driving him away from Christ. There are a lot of unsaved husbands using their wives as excuses not to follow Christ.

Submission is much more than just doing what someone asks. Peter said, **While they behold your chaste conversation coupled with fear.** The word **conversation** is simply an old English word that means behavior. It speaks not of what one says with his lips, but what he says with his life. Peter is saying to these wives that it is not enough to talk Christianity, they had to live it. There are a lot of women who have a good talk at Church, but they are devils at home. Peter speaks of a behavior that is **coupled with fear.** The wife's submission is **coupled** or connected to the fear of God. The wife submits out of her fear and reverence for God. The fear of God here means that the wife stands in awe and reverence of God to the point that she obeys Him. This speaks of the attitude behind the act. Submission is much more than just obeying. Submission is an attitude that results in an action. When your husband asks for a hot breakfast and you respond with, *"Well I'll set your cornflakes on fire tomorrow morning."* That may be submission, but the attitude behind it says, *"I'll show you, you may get a hot breakfast, but you won't enjoy it."* Biblical submission on the other hand says, *"I'll get up early and fix you some homemade biscuits, gravy and eggs."* Why? Because she loves the Lord with all of her heart and that is what He wants her to do. She has the right attitude behind her actions and when the husband sees that, he begins to think, *"Maybe there is something to this Christianity after all."*

HER BEAUTY IS INTERNAL

Whose adorning let it not be that outward adorning of plaiting the hair, and of wearing of gold, or of putting on of apparel. (1 Peter 3:3) Here is a verse that has been used to build a lot man made standards. Some poor misinformed husbands have taken this verse to mean that women ought to plain and drab. Such a notion is contrary to Scripture.

> **Thy cheeks are comely with rows of jewels, thy neck with chains of gold. (Song of Songs 1:10)**

> **Thy lips, O my spouse, drop as the honeycomb: honey and milk are under thy tongue; and the smell of thy garments is like the smell of Lebanon. (Song of Songs 4:11)**

> **How beautiful are thy feet with shoes, O prince's daughter! the joints of thy thighs are like jewels, the work of the hands of a cunning workman. (Song of Songs 7:1)**

This passage cannot be used to teach that a woman should never dress up or wear jewelry. Peter is not arguing against wearing jewelry as some suppose. In fact, he uses the adorning of **the holy women** and **Sara** as an illustration of submission and adornment. When we go back to the days of Abraham and Sara we quickly discover that the women had no problem wearing jewelry. In chapter 24 of Genesis we have the account of Abraham sending his servant to find a wife for Isaac. Notice the servant presented Rebekah with **a golden earring of half a shekel weight, and two bracelets for her hands of ten shekels weight of gold. (Genesis 24:22)** A little later he **brought forth jewels of silver, and jewels of gold, and raiment, and gave them to Rebekah: he gave also to her brother and to her mother precious things. (Genesis 24:53)** This passage cannot be used to impose legalistic restrictions against a woman adorning herself, rather it can be used in favor of it.

But let it be the hidden man of the heart, in that which is not corruptible, even the ornament of a meek and quiet spirit, which is in the sight of God of great price. (1 Peter 3:4) What Peter is saying is that inward beauty is far more important than outward adorning. Anyone can decorate the outside, but if the inside is ugly what good is it. This was Solomon's thought when he said, **As a jewel of gold in a swine's snout, so is a fair woman which is without discretion. (Proverbs 11:22)** For a rebellious woman to waste money on gold and silver and beautiful clothes is like dressing up a hog in nice clothes and fancy jewelry. On the inside it is still a hog and will head for the slop and mire as soon as it gets a chance. Peter is arguing that what truly wins a husband is inner beauty.

HER BLESSING IS ILLUSTRATED

For after this manner in the old time the holy women also, who trusted in God, adorned themselves, being in subjection unto their own husbands: Even as Sara obeyed Abraham, calling him lord: whose daughters ye are, as long as ye do well, and are not afraid with any

amazement. (1 Peter 3:5-6) The Lord blesses women who follow the biblical pattern in the home. Peter uses Sara and the women of old as examples of wives submitting to their husbands. He is simply saying that as God's people we do things differently from the world. By Divine requirement men have always been the leaders and women have always followed their leadership. This practice is as old as man's history with God. It is God Himself who established and set up the home. The biblical view of the husband-wife relationship is rejected by the Women's Liberation Movement, but it is God's way never the less.

HER BALANCE IS IMPORTANT

Let's remember that a wife's submission never exceeds Biblical boundaries. There have been some husbands so foolish as to expect their wives to do as they are told whether it is in line with the word of God or not. Only a fool would require that his wife disobey God and sin for him. The wife is to never do anything that is sinful. Her submission is to be **as unto the Lord. (Ephesians 5:22)** Just like Christ would never command His Church to do wrong, the husband is not to require of his wife that which would displease the Lord.

The Husband Who Wins His Wife
1 Peter 3:7

Peter now addresses Christian husbands. The exhortation is more brief than his instruction to wives, but not any less important. In fact, the greater responsibility is laid upon the husband. Peter addresses the husbands by once again using the word likewise. You will remember from our last study that the word **likewise** means *"after the same manner; in a similar way."* In this case as well, the husband is to submit to the God's plan. The husband is given clear instruction as to how he is to treat his wife. The husband is just as duty bound to fulfill his particular role in the marriage, as the wife is to fulfill hers.

THE DUTY THAT MUST BE ACKNOWLEDGED

Peter says, **ye husbands, dwell with them according to knowledge. (1 Peter 3:7a)** The word **dwell** carries the idea of *"togetherness."* It expresses the idea of *"living with someone in intimacy."* The husband and wife are not to be two different people, with different agendas living at the same residence. Instead they are a unit—they are one. Husbands, dwelling with your wife means more than sharing the same address or sleeping in the same bed with her. Many a couple get their mail out of the same box, but they don't dwell together. Too many husbands look at home as just a place to eat dinner and get a change of clothes before heading for a night with the boys. Men, coming in woofing down your dinner and then piling up on the couch is not dwelling with your wife. The idea is that we are not just roommates, we are partners together.

Our dwelling with our wife is to be **according to knowledge.** This knowledge here not only refers to the knowledge of God's plan for the home. But it also speaks of the knowledge you have of your wife. When you dwell with your wife like you are supposed to you get to know her. You get to know her desires and her goals. You even get to know her frustrations. You learn her weaknesses and her strengths. You know what she is like emotionally, and spiritually. This isn't academic knowledge, but rather a deep understanding of your wife's heart. It is knowing what makes her tick. A reporter once asked Mrs. Albert Einstein if she understood Dr. Einstein's theory of Relativity. She replied with somewhat of a twinkle in her eye, "*I do not understand his theory, but I do understand the doctor."* That is the idea here. Peter is telling us to get to know and understanding our wives.

THE DIFFERENCE THAT MUST BE ACCEPTED

Next Peter instructs, **giving honour unto the wife, as unto the weaker vessel. (1 Peter 3:7b)** There are three important thoughts here that we need to get a hold of.

First, consider **giving.** The word **giving** means "*to give, to deliver, to apportion, or to bestow."* The idea is the giving of a free gift. Too many husbands have the attitude that they honor their wives only if their own demands are fulfilled. This is a breakdown in the leadership role of the husband. Instead of leading her, he is holding her hostage to get his demands met. I've seen a lot of homes operated this way and they are miserable places. The husband is to freely bestow honor upon his wife whether or not he thinks she deserves it. God has commanded it and therefore, the husband owes it.

Second, consider her **honour.** The word **honour** means to "*esteem as precious.*" It carries the idea of holding her in high esteem. To honor your wife is to treat her as something that is very valuable and precious. **Whoso findeth a wife findeth a good thing, and obtaineth favour of the LORD. (Proverbs 18:22)** Husband, you have a wife because God has favored you. Honor her as a gift from the Lord.

Third, consider her as the **weaker vessel.** What does Peter mean by the woman being the **weaker vessel.** We know Peter doesn't mean weaker spiritually for later he explains that we are heirs together of the grace of life. In many cases, the wife is the more spiritual one in the marriage. Certainly, Peter doesn't mean weaker intellectually. We went to school with girls and we know they are pretty smart when test time comes. So then, what does Peter mean?

Well the word **wife** tells us exactly what he means. The word here translated **wife** is not from the exact same word that Peter used earlier in the text. This word carries the idea of *the feminine one.* We are to give honor unto our wife because she is the feminine one. That is, she is the delicate one. The idea here is not that she is less valuable, but that she is more valuable. Husbands, we are to honor our wife because of her great value. In their book, *The Gift Of Honor,*

Gary Smalley and John Trent have this to say about the word honor.

> "In ancient writings, honor was something of substance—literally heavy, valuable, costly, even priceless. For Homer, the Greek scholar wrote, 'The greater the cost of the gift, the more the honor' .. it is also used for someone who occupies a highly respected position in our lives, someone high on the priority list."

The thought that Peter is trying to get across here is that the more expensive and valuable a vessel, the more delicate and fragile it is. Wives, you are delicate and priceless work.

THE DESIGN THAT MUST BE APPRECIATED

Peter says, **as being heirs together of the grace of life. (1 Peter 3:7c)** This was radical thinking for the times in which Peter was speaking. Ninety-nine percent of the men of that day would not have agreed with Peter, yet he spoke by Divine Inspiration. In Peter's culture the idea of a woman being spiritually equal to men was not accepted. Being heirs together of God's grace never entered into their thinking. Secular history points this out. Greek and Roman women did not worship with men. In the orthodox Jewish synagogues, women had no place at all. They were not allowed to even be present. In Moslem countries women still are not allowed to worship with the men. They are separated from men in the mosques and removed as far from the center of the mosque as possible, and yet still be in the building. Peter does away with such nonsense and requires the Christian husband to fully accept the spiritual equality of his wife as one who is an heir of grace of life with him.

THE DANGER THAT MUST BE AVOIDED

Lastly, Peter warns, **that your prayers be not hindered. (1 Peter 3:7d)** This is a startling statement. Peter reminds us that our relation with our wife affects our relationship with God. In his book, *I Call It Heresy,* A. W. Tozer wrote:

> "I suppose there are many Christian husbands whose prayers are not being answered and they can think up a lot of reasons. But the fact is that thoughtless husbands are simply big, overbearing clods when it comes to consideration of their wives.
>
> If the husband would get himself straightened out in his own mind and spirit and live with his wife according to knowledge, and treat her with the chivalry that belongs to her as the weaker vessel, remembering that she is actually his sister in Christ, his prayers would be answered in spite of the devil and all of the other reasons that he gives.
>
> A husband's spiritual problems do not lie in the Kremlin nor in the Vatican but in the heart of man himself—in his attitude and inability to resist the, temptation to grumble and growl and dominate!
>
> There is no place for that kind of male leadership in any Christian home. What the Bible calls for is proper and kindly recognition of the true relationships of under-standing and love,

and the acceptance of a spirit of cooperation between husband and wife."

Husbands need to understand that they cannot be right with God when they are not right with their wife. Paul said **Husbands, love your wives, even as Christ also loved the church, and gave himself for it. (Ephesians 5:25)** Peter here does not call upon husbands to love their wives, but rather to manifest that love. Words are sometimes too easy to utter. It is not mere words that Peter is looking for here, but the demonstration of the husband's love for his wife.

Living The Good Life
1 Peter 3:8-12

A lot of believers miss out on the good life because they fail to recognize God's presence and purpose in the trials of life. In this section Peter tells us how to **love life, and see good days.**

WE MUST HAVE THE RIGHT ATTITUDE

Finally, be ye all of one mind, having compassion one of another, love as brethren, be pitiful, be courteous. (1 Peter 3:8) Here Peter call for us to come to the right attitude about ourselves and others.

Concord

Peter says, **be ye all of one mind. (1 Peter 3:8a)** This is a call for unity and harmony among the brethren. To be of one mind is to be like minded—we are to think alike. Thinking determines direction. **For as he thinketh in his heart, so is he… (Proverbs 23:7)** Our actions are the fruit of our thinking. In Philippians Paul gives us the key to being like-minded. **Let this mind be in you, which was also in Christ Jesus. (Philippians 2:5)** If God's people would stay in the Scriptures and develop the mind of Christ, there would be harmony and unity. The early Church operated in harmony. The term one accord is used several times to speak of their unity. (Acts 1:14; 2:1; 2:46; 4:24, 31-37; Acts 5:12; 8:6; 15:25) Unfortunately, this is a concept that is foreign to the thinking of many believers. Especially in Fundamental

Churches where this general attitude is, Why get along when we can fight. Like Paul, we need to fight the good fight, but all of this fighting one another that we see today is contrary to God's plan. His desire is that we get along and get the job done. This does not advocate a lack of biblical separation. But it does require unity in the local Church and among the brethren. **Behold, how good and how pleasant it is for brethren to dwell together in unity!. (Psalms 133:1)**

Compassion

Peter says, **having compassion one of another. (1 Peter 3:8b)** Compassion comes from the word "*soompathace*" and carries the idea "*feeling with or having the same feelings.*" We get our word sympathy from it. It is not simply feeling pity, but identifying with the hurts and heartaches of other. **Rejoice with them that do rejoice, and weep with them that weep. (Romans 12:15)**

Paul expands this telling us to **love as brethren. (1 Peter 3:8c)** We hear a lot of talk about love, but what we see is not the love of the Bible. Love is an action word. Jesus Christ put principle into picture. **But God commendeth his love toward us, in that, while we were yet sinners, Christ died for us. (Romans 5:8)** If you want to see true and pure love—look at Christ. We are to go beyond the knowledge and profession of love and demonstrate our love in our dealings with others. Jesus said **This is my commandment, That ye love one another, as I have loved you. (John 15:12)** Jesus gave love a new standard. Grace always carries a greater responsibility than law. The law said, **thou shalt love thy neighbour as thyself. (Leviticus 19:18)** The command to love one another was new in the sense that Jesus gave it a new standard. No longer do we love each other as we love ourselves, but Jesus commanded us to, **love one another; as I have loved you. (John 13:34)** Jesus Christ loved us all the way to the cross. **Greater love hath no man than this, that a man lay down his life for his friends. (John 15:13)** It is one thing to say I love you, but it is quite another to show it. God not only said I love you; He demonstrated His love for us. Jesus left us with the responsibility to love one another the same way. Jesus also said, **By this shall all men know that ye are my disciples, if ye have love one to another. (John 13:35)** In our love for one another the world should see God's love for them. Our love for each other is evidence that we are His disciples.

Caring

Peter says **be pitiful.** Now I've seen a lot of pitiful people, even many pitiful Christians, but that's not what Peter is talking about here. The word **pitiful** carries the idea of being *"good heartedness, full of pity, tenderhearted."* The idea is that our heart is to be soft, sensitive and sympathetic toward the needs of others. The same word is used twelve times in the Gospels to describe the response of Christ to the suffering and heartache caused by sin.

Courteous

We are to **be courteous.** This word carries the idea of being *"humble minded".* Being humble means having an honest estimation of oneself before God. It is the opposite of pride. When we are humble, we realize that we all came out of the same pit and saved by the same grace. Right thinking about what we are will produce a right relationship with others.

Not only must we have the **Right Attitude**, but …

WE MUST HAVE THE RIGHT ACTIONS

Not rendering evil for evil, or railing for railing: but contrariwise blessing; knowing that ye are thereunto called, that ye should inherit a blessing. (1 Peter 3:9) Having dealt with our attitude, Peter now deals with how we respond to each other.

First, Peter says, **Not rendering evil for evil.** The world's way is to strike back. Get even! But the Christian way is forgiveness. Jesus said, **Ye have heard that it hath been said, An eye for an eye, and a tooth for a tooth: But I say unto you, That ye resist not evil: but whosoever shall smite thee on thy right cheek, turn to him the other also. And if any man will sue thee at the law, and take away thy coat, let him have thy cloke also. And whosoever shall compel thee to go a mile, go with him twain. (Matthew 5:38-41)** Once again, grace demands more of us than the law did. On one occasion Peter came to Jesus and asked, **Lord, how oft shall my brother sin against me, and I forgive him? till seven times? Jesus saith unto him, I say not unto thee, Until seven times: but, Until seventy times seven. (Matthew 18:21-22)** Peter thought that he was going the extra mile in offering to forgive an erring brother **seven times.** However, man's ways are not God's ways and our Lord took the opportunity to teach the important truth of unlimited forgiveness of others. Peter is basically asking, *"When my* *brother sins against me, how many times do I have to forgive him? Will seven times be enough?"* Jesus answered, **I say not unto thee, Until seven times: but, Until seventy times seven.** Jesus was not saying that we are to forgive only 490 times, but that our forgiveness is to be unconditional and unlimited. Forgiveness is more than an act; it is an attitude. As a child of God my spirit is to be one of love and forgiveness. Like God's forgiveness, our forgiveness is to reach beyond the offences of others. **And be ye kind one to another, tenderhearted, forgiving one another, even as God for Christ's sake hath forgiven you. (Ephesians 4:32)** We do not deal with others according to some set of rules and laws, but with grace. It is a limitless forgiveness, just as God forgives His children.

Second, we are not to return **railing for railing.** The word **railing** speaks of *"cursing, speaking evil of, abusive, and insulting talk."* Railing comes from the root of the word reviled used earlier in connection with Christ. **Who, when he was reviled, reviled not again; when he suffered, he threatened not; but committed himself to him that judgeth righteously. (1 Peter 2:23)** This kind of speech has no place in the believer's life. **Let no corrupt communication proceed out of your mouth, but that which is good to the use of edifying, that it may minister grace unto the hearers. (Ephesians 4:29)**

Peter says, **but contrariwise blessing; knowing that ye are thereunto called, that ye should inherit a blessing.** Instead of cussing them, bless those who cuss you. Paul said, **being reviled, we bless. (1 Corinthians 4:12)** This was the teaching of our Saviour. **But I say unto you, Love your**

enemies, bless them that curse you, do good to them that hate you, and pray for them which despitefully use you, and persecute you. (Matthew 5:44) We are not be running around cussing and ripping people apart.

Third, Peter says, **let him refrain his tongue from evil, and his lips that they speak no guile. (1 Peter 3:10)** In the last verse Peter dealt with how we speak to others, now he deals with our speech in general. Paul commanded us to put away, **evil speaking. (Ephesians 4:31)** The tongue is the index of the heart. James said, **If any man among you seem to be religious, and bridleth not his tongue, but deceiveth his own heart, this man's religion is vain. (James 1:26)** If a man claims to be a mature Christian but can't keep his own tongue from corrupt communication, he has already identified himself as deceived and his religion is vain. James went on to say, **And the tongue is a fire, a world of iniquity: so is the tongue among our members, that it defileth the whole body, and setteth on fire the course of nature; and it is set on fire of hell. (James 3:6)** A loose and smoldering tongue is not lit with any ordinary fire, it is **set on fire of hell.** The work of the uncontrolled tongue is a product of hell. A man who cannot control his tongue is doing the Devil's work. **An hypocrite with his mouth destroyeth his neighbour. (Proverbs 11:9)** Understand that Contentious, Critical, Careless, and Corrupt communication is the work of a wicked tongue. Like the poison of a viper, the tongue is armed with the lethal venom of hate, hostility, and destructive words of death. **Their throat is an open sepulchre; with their tongues they have used deceit; the poison of asps is under their lips: Whose mouth is full of** cursing and bitterness. (Romans 3:13-14) Corrupt communication has no place in the Christian life.

Fourth, **Let him eschew evil, and do good; let him seek peace, and ensue it. (1 Peter 3:11a)** The word **eschew** means *"to shun, to avoid, go out of the way."* The idea is that we are to work at shunning, avoiding and going out of the way of wickedness. We must live the separated Christian life. We don't hear much about separation today. Many actually ridicule the though of separation. However, we must realize that biblical separation is based upon one of God's essential attributes—HIS HOLINESS. God never intended for separation to result in a sect of Pharisaism, but rather a holy priesthood of believers. **But as he which hath called you is holy, so be ye holy in all manner of conversation. (1 Peter 1:15)** Christ's intention when He saved us was to **redeem us from all iniquity, and purify unto himself a peculiar people, zealous of good works. (Titus 2:14)** The Bible is clear on the matter of separation. (2 Corinthians 6:14-18) Separation is a principle set forth by Almighty God for the purpose of protecting His people.

Fifth, we are to **seek peace, and ensue it. (1 Peter 3:11)** True peace can be known only by God's people. The lost have no real peace. **There is no peace, saith the LORD, unto the wicked. (Isaiah 48:22)** They do however search for peace, but it is a false peace. **For when they shall say, Peace and safety; then sudden destruction cometh upon them, as travail upon a woman with child; and they shall not escape. (1 Thessalonians 5:3)** Where God has not worked and divine grace transformed the heart there is no real peace. **Therefore being justified by faith, we have peace**

with God through our Lord Jesus Christ: By whom also we have access by faith into this grace wherein we stand, and rejoice in hope of the glory of God. (Romans 5:1-2)

It is sad that many believers have no peace. But notice that Peter says we are to **ensue** peace. This word ensue speaks of going after something with an intense effort. It carries the idea of being aggressive in a hunt. Paul talked about a peace that would exceed even our understanding. **Be careful for nothing; but in every thing by prayer and supplication with thanksgiving let your requests be made known unto God. And the peace of God, which passeth all understanding, shall keep your hearts and minds through Christ Jesus. (Philippians 4:6-7)** That's the kind of peace we need.

We must have the **Right Attitude**, the **Right Actions** and ...

WE MUST HAVE THE RIGHT AIM

For the eyes of the Lord are over the righteous, and his ears are open unto their prayers: but the face of the Lord is against them that do evil. (1 Peter 3:12) Our aim ought to be to please God. Remember that the context of 1st Peter is suffering and persecution. Peter is stressing the fact that God's eyes see us and His ears hear our prayers. Peter says, **The face of the Lord is against them that do evil.** He is quoting from Psalm 34:16 where the context is God's judgment on the wicked. The idea is simple. We are to please God and let Him take care of judging those who persecute us.

How To Be Used Of God
1 Peter 3:13-17

Here is a subject that ought to be the concern of every believer. Every Christian is saved to serve. Not everyone will be a Pastor, Evangelist, Deacon or Sunday-school teacher, but everyone in the local Church ought to have a place of service. Peter lists several prerequisites for being successful in Christian service.

A STEADFAST CONFIDENCE

And who is he that will harm you, if ye be followers of that which is good?. (1 Peter 3:13) Folks stumble at this verse because they are looking at the temporal rather than the eternal. Too many Christians focus on the here and now rather than the "there and then." Peter is not saying that if we are good no one will hurt us. The very theme of this book is *Suffering For Christ.* The bottom line is that we will suffer for living the Christian life. However, Peter asks this rhetorical question to draw our attention to the fact that believers are in the providential care of God. God sovereignly cares for His own and no one can harm us unless God allows it. Shadrach, Meshach, and Abednego were cast into the furnace. Daniel was thrown into lion's den. Jeremiah was put in the stocks. Elijah was persecuted by Jezebel. Even the great Apostle Paul spoke of the hardships of service:

> **Are they ministers of Christ? (I speak as a fool) I am more; in labours more abundant, in stripes above measure, in prisons more frequent, in deaths oft. Of the Jews five times received I forty stripes save one.**

Thrice was I beaten with rods, once was I stoned, thrice I suffered shipwreck, a night and a day I have been in the deep; In journeyings often, in perils of waters, in perils of robbers, in perils by mine own countrymen, in perils by the heathen, in perils in the city, in perils in the wilderness, in perils in the sea, in perils among false brethren; In weariness and painfulness, in watchings often, in hunger and thirst, in fastings often, in cold and nakedness. (2 Corinthians 11:23-27)

Anyone who lives all out for Christ will not have an easy ride. Peter is not telling us that we will not suffer, but that ultimately there will be no harm to us. There can be no lasting harm to the righteous because, **we know that all things work together for good to them that love God, to them who are the called according to his purpose. (Romans 8:28)** Anything they do to us only moves us closer to being with Christ. **Who shall separate us from the love of Christ? shall tribulation, or distress, or persecution, or famine, or nakedness, or peril, or sword?. (Romans 8:35)** Paul was later beheaded for his faith, but it didn't harm him. It only ushered him into the presence of Christ which was **far better. (Philippians 1:23)** The exemption Peter was talking about was not freedom from difficulty, but rather freedom from defeat.

A SATISFIED CONDITION

Peter says, **if ye be followers of that which is good? (1 Peter 3:13)** The word **followers** carries the idea of "*one who burns with zeal or a zealot."* It speaks of the Christian who is deeply devoted and firmly committed to Jesus Christ. In the next verse Peter says, **But and if ye suffer for**

righteousness' sake, happy are ye: and be not afraid of their terror, neither be troubled. (1 Peter 3:14) God's people have always faced persecution for righteousness' sake. But regardless of the persecution Peter says, **happy are ye.** Jesus said, **Blessed are ye, when men shall revile you, and persecute you, and shall say all manner of evil against you falsely, for my sake. Rejoice, and be exceeding glad: for great is your reward in heaven: for so persecuted they the prophets which were before you. (Matthew 5:11-12)** The believer can suffer differently from anyone else. Because of our relationship with Christ our whole outlook is different. We can suffer and be happy all at the same time. A martyr in Switzerland was standing barefoot and tied to the stake, about to be burned to death for his faith. He called to the magistrate who was overseeing his execution and asked him to come near. As the executioner came close, the Christian said with confidence, *"I am about to be burned to death for faith in my Lord Jesus Christ. Lay your hand on my heart. If it beats any faster than it ordinarily beats, don't believe in my Christ."* What a powerful testimony!

Polycarp, bishop of Smyrna, was one of the first martyrs to die for Christ. At 86 years of age Polycarp was pressured by the Roman proconsul to renounce Christ and be set free. He answered, *"Eighty and six years have I served Him and He never did me any injury. How then can I blaspheme my King and my Savior?"* They tied him to a stake, piled the wood high and set it afire, but long before his suffering body was reduced to ashes, his triumphant soul was at home with his Saviour. Paul had the same kind of holy contentment. While sitting in a Roman prison awaiting execution he said, **And the Lord shall deliver me from every evil work, and will preserve me unto his heavenly kingdom: to whom be glory** for ever and ever. Amen. (2 Timothy 4:18) These were men who were **followers of that which is good.** They were sold out to Christ and His cause. Therefore, they were happy with whatever came their way. So many Christian fail to enjoy this truth because they live for the world rather than for their Saviour.

A SANCTIFIED CONSECRATION

But sanctify the Lord God in your hearts. (1 Peter 3:15a) Notice the contrast—**But.** Instead of allowing fear to take hold of your heart, allow God to fully occupy your heart. The word **sanctify** means *"to set apart."* According to Noah Webster, it is the *"act of separating from a common to a sacred use, or of devoting and dedicating a person or thing to the service and worship of God."* We are in the world but not of the world. We are not to settle down and be at home in this world. This is a truth that runs throughout the Word of God. **Love not the world, neither the things that are in the world. If any man love the world, the love of the Father is not in him. (1 John 2:15)** The word **world** comes from the Greek word *"kosmos,"* meaning *"arrangement or decoration"* and speaks of this world's order or system. Adam and Eve's sin resulted in a curse upon the earth bringing it under the control of Satan. Everything about this world system is therefore, anti-God. **For all that is in the world, the lust of the flesh, and the lust of the eyes, and the pride of life, is not of the Father, but is of the world. (1 John 2:16)** The programs, pursuits, practices, purposes, and philosophies of this wicked world are the result of fallen man's ambitions and desires as he follows the leadership of Satan. This is in direct opposition with the purpose and plan of God for man. If we are not careful we will allow the world to captivate our heart. Instead we are to sanctify God in our heart.

To sanctify the Lord God in your heart means that you give Him first place. Notice that this is heart matter. This is not talking about spiffing things up on the outside. This is talking about getting things thoroughly right and making Christ Lord in the heart where it really counts. Once the believer sanctifies Christ in his heart, things will get right on the outside.

A SCRIPTURAL CONVICTION

Next we are to, **be ready always to give an answer to every man that asketh you a reason of the hope that is in you with meekness and fear. (1 Peter 3:15b)** Testifying for Christ is a fulltime business. Peter tell us to **be ready always.** Believers re to be ready at any time to share Christ. There are a lot of missed opportunities because God's people are not ready to witness to the lost. And what are we to be ready for? Peter says, **to give an answer.** The word for answer is *"apologia."* We get or word apologetics from it. It is a judicial term used to describe a formal defense in a court of law (Acts 25:16; 2 Timothy 4:16). When people ask us why we are a Christians, we are to be ready and able to tell them why.

A SOUND CONSCIENCE

Having a good conscience; that, whereas they speak evil of you, as of evildoers, they may be ashamed that falsely accuse your good conversation in Christ. (1 Peter 3:16) It is absolutely essential to have a good conscience before God and man if we are going to be used in God's service. A good conscience is the certain knowledge that our life is in line with the will of God and our actions are pleasing to Him. Job is good example. He didn't understand the details of his suffering, but he had a clear conscience before God. When his friends betrayed him and falsely accused him of being in sin Job rested in the fact that his heart and walk was right before God. **But he knoweth the way that I take: when he hath tried me, I shall come forth as gold. (Job 23:10)** Job lived for God and God was his witness.

Peter has just commanded us to be ready to give an answer for the hope that is in us. Now he tells us to have a **good conscience.** Peter is telling us that if we are going to win people to Christ we must live what we speak. People need more than mere words, they need examples. Slick talk and super salesmanship evangelism does not produce converts. Christians who live their convictions will have greater opportunities to win people to Christ.

A SETTLING CERTAINTY

For it is better, if the will of God be so, that ye suffer for well doing, than for evil doing. (1 Peter 3:17) Peter simply states that it is better to suffer for doing what is right than to suffer for sin. Sometimes is God's will that we suffer persecution. Though we don't like it, suffering can be good for us in several ways. When we handle it right God get glory from our lives. During hard times we have the tendency to draw closer to God.

The Triumphant Christ
1 Peter 3:18-22

At the heart of the gospel is the fact that Jesus Christ, who knew no sin, died for sinners. Peter closes this section on the unjust suffering of believers with the example of how Christ suffered unjustly to redeem the lost.

THE SUFFERING HE DEMONSTRATED

For Christ also hath once suffered for sins, the just for the unjust, that he might bring us to God, being put to death in the flesh, but quickened by the Spirit. (1 Peter 3:18) The previous verse declares that it could be the will of God that we suffer for well doing. Now Peter gives the greatest example of suffering, the Lord Jesus Christ himself.

The Reach

For Christ also hath once suffered for sins. Never before had there been a sacrifice like this one. Thousands upon thousands of sacrifices were made in the Old Testament. These sacrifices could not accomplish that which man needed most—a sacrifice that would fully and finally cover his sin and make an atonement for his soul. With the sacrificial system of the Old Testament there was always the need for another sacrifice. But that all changed when Jesus Christ, the Lamb of God, was sacrificed upon Calvary's altar. Peter said that Jesus Christ **once suffered for sins.** His atoning death forever eliminated the need for further sacrifices. When He died the price for sin was fully paid once and for all by His shed blood. Paul drives this point home several times in the book of Hebrews. (Hebrews 7:26-27; 9:24-28; 10:10-14)

The word **once** comes from *hapax* and according to Vines, speaks of *perpetual validity, not requiring repetition.* It carries the idea of *once for all.* This was a new concept to the Jews. They had slaughtered millions of animals over the years. During the Passover alone, as many as a quarter million sheep would be slaughtered and offered as sacrifices. But the sacrificial death of Jesus Christ ended all of that. In Jesus' final moment on the cross, **he said, It is finished: and he bowed his head, and gave up the ghost. (John 19:30)** When He said it is finished He meant that sin was paid for fully and finally. **For in that he died, he died unto sin once: but in that he liveth, he liveth unto God. (Romans 6:10)** Jesus defeated all sin for all sinners for all time. There is not need for any other sacrifice because his sacrifice was sufficient for everyone and accepted by God.**Who being the brightness of his glory, and the express image of his person, and upholding all things by the word of his power, when he had by himself purged our sins, sat down on the right hand of the Majesty on high. (Hebrews 1:3)**

The Representation

When Christ died He was representing us—the sinner. The Lord Jesus died, **the just for the unjust.** Jesus Christ died in our place. We deserved to die, not Him. He is the just and righteous God of Heaven. We are wicked sinners. He never sinned. We sin continually. **For he hath made him to be sin**

for us, who knew no sin; that we might be made the righteousness of God in him. (2 Corinthians 5:21) Jesus Christ took the sinner's place. He died instead of me. He died to pay for my sins, not His.

> **But we see Jesus, who was made a little lower than the angels for the suffering of death, crowned with glory and honour; that he by the grace of God should taste death for every man. (Hebrews 2:9)**

Notice it says that He died for **every man**. Not just for Calvin's elect, but every man. The Bible says that God is **not willing that any should perish, but that all should come to repentance. (2 Peter 3:9)** God does not want anyone in Hell, He wants all men to be saved. There are no exceptions. Christ died for all. He is **the Lamb of God, which taketh away the sin of the world. (John 1:29)** Again, it is not the sin of the elect, but the **sin of the world**. In His death He represented every man, woman and child to enter this world—past, present or future.

The Reconciliation

The Bible says Jesus died, **that he might bring us to God.** The words **bring us to** means *"to lead before, to bring into the presence of, to bring to."* It carries the idea of being lead into the presence of and being presented to the King. At the court of kings in Bible days there was an official called the Prosagogeus. He could either grant or deny access to the king. He decided who would be admitted into the king's presence. In other words, he held the power of access to the king's presence. For the sinner Jesus Christ is the Prosagogeus—He alone holds the power of access into the

Father's presence. **For through him we both have access by one Spirit unto the Father. (Ephesians 2:18)** Jesus Christ gives us access into the presence of God. **By whom also we have access by faith into this grace wherein we stand, and rejoice in hope of the glory of God. (Romans 5:2)**

The Resurrection

Jesus was **put to death in the flesh, but quickened by the Spirit.** His physical body died. He stopped breathing. His heart stopped beating. Infidels and critics have attacked the resurrection of Christ by claiming He never really died on the cross. Their claim is that He merely fainted and that coolness of the tomb revived Him, then he simply got up and walked back out into the world. However, Peter clearly states that Jesus was **put to death in the flesh.** In order to hasten their deaths, you will remember that the executioners broke the legs of the two thieves crucified along side of Christ. (John 19:31–32) However, the Bible says, **But when they came to Jesus, and saw that he was dead already, they brake not his legs. (John 19:33)**

His physical body died. But Praise God the Bible says, **He was quickened by the Spirit.** The word **quickened** means *to make alive.* God Almighty, through the power of the Holy Spirit, restored the physical life of Jesus Christ at the resurrection. The Bible speaks of Jesus **Whom God hath raised up, having loosed the pains of death: because it was not possible that he should be holden of it. (Acts 2:24)** While visiting Egypt, the Christian apologist, Dr. Harry Rimmer had an interesting conversation with a Muslim tour guide. As they discussed their different faiths Dr. Rimmer said, My faith believes that God has revealed Himself in three Persons. The Egyptian said, We believe that too. Dr. Rimmer continued, We believe that God has revealed Himself in creation, and the Egyptian agreed. Dr. Rimmer said, We believe that God has revealed Himself in a book, the Bible. The Muslim guide said, We believe God has revealed himself in a book, the Koran. We believe that God has revealed Himself in a Man, Jesus Christ, said Rimmer. And we believe He has revealed Himself in a man, Mohammed, was the response. Then Rimmer said, We believe that our Saviour rose from the dead. And the Egyptian said timidly, We honor Mohammed's tomb in Medina. Therein lies the difference between Christianity and every other religion in the world. Christians serve a risen Saviour! Three times at the grave of Jesus it is declared, **He is not here**. (Matthew 28:6, Mark 16:6, Luke 24:6)

Some sixty years after His resurrection, Jesus would proclaim to John on the isle of Patmos:

> **I am he that liveth, and was dead; and, behold, I am alive for evermore, Amen; and have the keys of hell and of death. (Revelation 1:18)**

Christians are the only people who can sing the song, "*I Serve A Risen Saviour.*" Just like Jesus' life was restored at the resurrection. Jesus restores our physical life for eternity when we come to Him for salvation.

> **But if the Spirit of him that raised up Jesus from the dead dwell in you, he that raised up Christ from the dead shall also quicken your mortal bodies by his Spirit that dwelleth in you. (Romans 8:11)**

The resurrection of Jesus Christ is essential to the Christian life. **And if Christ be not risen, then is our preaching vain, and your faith is also vain. (1 Corinthians 15:14)**

THE SERMON HE DELIVERED

By which also he went and preached unto the spirits in prison. (1 Peter 3:19) There is a great deal of debate surrounding this verse. The debate centers around who these spirits are. Some interpret them as men, however, in the Bible men are not seen as spirits. It seems more reasonable to believe that these **spirits in prison** are fallen angels. Throughout Scripture angels are referred to as spirits.

According to Scripture, there is a place where evil spirits are confined. It is a place where they are held awaiting the judgment of God. Peter also refers to this place in his second letter.

> **For if God spared not the angels that sinned, but cast them down to hell, and delivered them into chains of darkness, to be reserved unto judgment. (2 Peter 2:4)**

Jude also speaks of these fallen angels.

> **And the angels which kept not their first estate, but left their own habitation, he hath reserved in everlasting chains under darkness unto the judgment of the great day. (Jude 1:6)**

The words **first estate** speak of *"place, rank or position."* These are angels that did not stay where God put them. In other words, these are the angels that initially sided with Satan and rebelled against God (Revelation 12:4) when he attempted to overthrow God and take His throne (Isaiah 14:12-15). In the 9th chapter of Revelation, when the fifth trumpet sounds these demons will be released from their prison as a judgment upon the wicked Christ-rejecting sinners of the Great Tribulation period.

So, what exactly does Peter mean when he says Christ **went and preached unto the spirits in prison?** After His resurrection and before his ascension into heaven, Jesus descended into to the heart of the earth and proclaimed victory. The herald of Christ's triumphant victory was heard throughout the halls of Hell as Jesus proclaimed His defeat of Satan.

Once the proclamation of victory was made, Jesus gathered the saved of the Old Testament from Paradise and ascended to Heaven.

> **Wherefore he saith, When he ascended up on high, he led captivity captive, and gave gifts unto men. (Now that he ascended, what is it but that he also descended first into the lower parts of the earth? He that descended is the same also that ascended up far above all heavens, that he might fill all things) (Ephesians 4:8-10)**

Here is the illustration of a king who has been victorious in battle. He has conquered his enemy and is returning home in glory. The king is riding upon his white stallion, following is his army—his faithful soldiers. Behind them comes the enemy shacked in chains, defeated and helpless. Paul quotes part of Psalm 68:18, one of David's victories as an illustration. In this verse, we have a reference to one of David's victories in liberating a number of captives who had been taken out of Israel. David brought those captives back in triumph and in victory to reunite them to their people and their homeland. David captured those who were in captivity and brought them home. Paul takes that historical account and uses it as an illustration of Christ's victorious ascension. He uses the same illustration in Colossians speaking of Christ's victory over the principalities and powers of darkness. **And having spoiled principalities and powers, he made a show of them openly, triumphing over them in it. (Colossians 2:15)** When Christ ascended up on high, He did so as a mighty and victorious King.

Notice that Jesus **also descended first into the lower parts of the earth.** What does that mean? A lot of folks seem to stumble over this one, but I believe the Bible gives us the answer. During these New Testament times when a believer dies he goes straight into the presence of God. **For I am in a strait betwixt two, having a desire to depart, and to be with Christ; which is far better. (Philippians 1:23)** Paul spoke of death as departing and being with Christ. Later he said, **We are confident, I say, and willing rather to be absent from the body, and to be present with the Lord. (2 Corinthians 5:8)** Clearly the New Testament teaches that those who die in Christ go immediately to be with Him.

However, in the Old Testament that was not the case. We see this clearly in Jesus' teaching on the rich man and Lazarus. (Luke 16:22-26) Jesus said that when Lazarus died, he was carried by the angels to a place called Abraham's

The Triumphant Life

bosom. However, the rich man also died, and he was buried, and in hell he lifted up his eyes being in torments. We also learn that Lazarus and the rich man could see one another. We see that one place was a place of comfort while the other was a place torment. The rich man could speak to Abraham, and Abraham could speak to him. (vs 24-25) These two places were in close proximity to each other, the only thing that separated the two was a great impassable gulf. (26) So then, there was **Abraham's bosom,** that was Paradise where the saved went as we see in Lazarus's case. Then there was the **Hell** side where lost people like the rich man went. After Jesus paid the price for sin the saved people in Paradise were given access directly into Heaven. They could now be in the very presence of God.

Many ask Why go through all of this? Why couldn't they just go to Heaven when they died since they were saved? Because the price of their redemption had not been paid. It had been promised and they, by faith believed God and were saved. **Even as Abraham believed God, and it was accounted to him for righteousness. (Galatians 3:6)** People in the Old Testament were saved by believing in the coming Messiah. But until the Messiah came and paid the price of redemption, there could be no entrance into Heaven. No one can stand in the presence of God without his sin being paid for first. This leading of the captivity had to have taken place sometime after the resurrection. At the point when Mary discovered Jesus in the garden He had not yet ascended to Heaven. **Jesus saith unto her, Touch me not; for I am not yet ascended to my Father: but go to my brethren, and say unto them, I ascend unto my Father, and your Father; and** to my God, and your God. (John 20:17)** It was sometime after the resurrection that Jesus descended into the lower parts of the earth and made the glorious announcement that the sin debt had been paid—the Saviour is victorious. What a time of shouting that must have been when Jesus pronounced Satan's defeat and gathered His saved out of the paradise side of Sheol and like the mighty victorious King who had just defeated the enemy and liberated his captives, led them into the presence of God.

THE SALVATION HE DESCRIBES

Which sometime were disobedient, when once the longsuffering of God waited in the days of Noah, while the ark was a preparing, wherein few, that is, eight souls were saved by water. The like figure whereunto even baptism doth also now save us. (not the putting away of the filth of the flesh, but the answer of a good conscience toward God,) by the resurrection of Jesus Christ. (1 Peter 3:20-21) There are at least three thoughts in these verses.

God's Patience

The **longsuffering of God waited.** Longsuffering is one of God's great attributes. **But thou, O Lord, art a God full of compassion, and gracious, longsuffering, and plenteous in mercy and truth. (Psalm 86:15)** Longsuffering carries the idea of being patient and slow to anger. Jesus, when He could have summoned **more than twelve legions of angels. (Matthew 26:53)** to His side, instead, **endured the cross. (Hebrews 12:2)** Later He prayed for their forgiveness. **Then said Jesus, Father, forgive them; for they know not what they do. And they parted his raiment, and cast lots. (Luke

23:34) God is so longsuffering. When He could rightfully judge and cast us into Hell, He waits for our repentance.

God's Provision

Peter says that God waited, **while the ark was a preparing.** God had pronounced judgment upon the wickedness of man even to the destruction of the world. **And GOD saw that the wickedness of man was great in the earth, and that every imagination of the thoughts of his heart was only evil continually. And it repented the LORD that he had made man on the earth, and it grieved him at his heart. And the LORD said, I will destroy man whom I have created from the face of the earth; both man, and beast, and the creeping thing, and the fowls of the air; for it repenteth me that I have made them. (Genesis 6:5-7)** There would be no reprieve. Judgment was coming, but God made provision for those who would repent. The same is true of our day. We are living under imminent judgment. However, God has provided a way of escape from His judgment. **For God sent not his Son into the world to condemn the world; but that the world through him might be saved. He that believeth on him is not condemned: but he that believeth not is condemned already, because he hath not believed in the name of the only begotten Son of God. (John 3:17-18)** The only thing that holds God's judgment back is His desire that we accept His provision and be saved. (2 Peter 3:8-10)

God's Picture

Peter says, **wherein few, that is, eight souls were saved by water. The like figure whereunto even baptism doth**

also now save us. (not the putting away of the filth of the flesh, but the answer of a good conscience toward God,) by the resurrection of Jesus Christ. (1 Peter 3:20b-21) Those who teach baptismal regeneration get all excited about this verse. Their claim is that this passage proves that we must be baptized to be saved. As is with all false doctrine the Bible disproves it. Let's look at what the passage does say rather than what they say about it.

Notice that Peter says that baptism is a **figure.** In other words, it is not that baptism saves, but baptism is a figure or a type of salvation. Baptism gives us a picture of salvation. **Know ye not, that so many of us as were baptized into Jesus Christ were baptized into his death? Therefore we are buried with him by baptism into death: that like as Christ was raised up from the dead by the glory of the Father, even so we also should walk in newness of life. (Romans 6:3-4)** Baptism pictures the death of the old man before we were saved, the burial of the old life, and the resurrection of the new life in Christ. Baptism is an outward expression of an inward reality. It identifies the person being baptized with Christ and says that a change has taken place in his heart and life.

The place of safety was in the ark not in the water. Noah's Ark was a type of Christ and His salvation.

1) **The Ark Was Provided By God, Through Grace. And God said unto Noah, The end of all flesh is come before me; for the earth is filled with violence through them; and, behold, I will destroy them with the earth. Make thee an ark of gopher wood; rooms shalt thou make in**

the ark, and shalt pitch it within and without with pitch. (Genesis 6:13-14)** God was sending judgment but in His mercy He provided a way of escape for any who would believe. This was an act of His grace. **Noah found grace in the eyes of the Lord. (Genesis 6:8)**

2) **The Ark Had Three Stories**. God said, **with lower, second, and third stories shalt thou make it. (Genesis 6:16)** The three stories would be typical of the Trinity. All three were involved in our salvation. God the Father provided His Son. God the Son died for us. God the Holy Spirit draws the lost to Christ.

3) **The Ark Had A Window Above**. **A window shalt thou make to the ark, and in a cubit shalt thou finish it above. (Genesis 6:16)** Noah's look was to be upward. His focus was not to be on the judgment around him, but on God Who delivers from judgment.

4) **The Ark Had Only One Door**. God said, **and the door of the ark shalt thou set in the side thereof. (Genesis 6:16)** There was only one way into the ark of salvation and that was through the door. This is a type of the Lord Jesus Christ. **I am the door: by me if any man enter in, he shall be saved…. (John 10:9)**

5) **There Was An Invitation Given**. **And the LORD said unto Noah, Come thou and all thy house into the ark…. (Genesis 7:1)** Just as God invited Noah into the ark, Jesus invites us to **Come unto me, all ye that labour and are heavy laden, and I will give you rest. (Matthew 11:28)**

6) They Were Secure In The Ark. **And they that went in, went in male and female of all flesh, as God had commanded him: and the LORD shut him in. (Genesis 7:16)** The Lord shut Noah in the ark and He kept him secure. We too are shut in when we get saved. **In whom ye also trusted, after that ye heard the word of truth, the gospel of your salvation: in whom also after that ye believed, ye were sealed with that holy Spirit of promise, Which is the earnest of our inheritance until the redemption of the purchased possession, unto the praise of his glory. (Ephesians 1:13-14)**

Peter simply goes back to Noah's day and uses it as an illustration of God's longsuffering and grace in saving the lost. The ark and Noah's family serves as a type of those who are in Christ.

THE SUPREMACY HE DESERVES

Who is gone into heaven, and is on the right hand of God; angels and authorities and powers being made subject unto him. (1 Peter 3:22) The Lord Jesus Christ is now seated at the right hand of the Father. The **right hand of God** is the place of supreme honor, power and authority. (Psalm 110:1; Ephesians 1:20; Colossians 3:1; Hebrews 8:1; 10:12; 12:2) All powers are subject unto Him. Angels, demons, even Satan himself is subject to our Lord.

Living In The Shadow Of Eternity
1 Peter 4:1-11

We are living in an extremely perverted age. Moral purity is fighting for its life. This world is steeped in its wicked debauchery as it seeks to serve and satisfy the desires of depravity. This could be expected from the world, but even many professing Christians have given in, surrendered to the moral contamination of the day.

Here in this section Peter reminds us that if we are going to have an impact on the people around us, we must be different from them. It is not easy to be different. It is not popular to be different. However, it is required that we be different. We must have a Holy Walk In A Hostile World. Peter gives us seven principles for Living In The Shadow Of Eternity.

PREPARATION

Forasmuch then as Christ hath suffered for us in the flesh, arm yourselves likewise with the same mind. (1 Peter 4:1a) The first step is preparation—we must be prepared for what is coming when we sell out to Christ and live whole heartedly for Him in a wicked world. Paul points us to Christ's example of Christian living. Peter reminds us that if we are going to live right there will be suffering. This is far from the blab it and grab it, peaches and cream philosophy of the prosperity gospel movement. No one ever lived better than Christ and no one ever suffered more. **He is**

despised and rejected of men; a man of sorrows, and acquainted with grief: and we hid as it were our faces from him; he was despised, and we esteemed him not. (Isaiah 53:3) The Bible describes in vivid detail the awful suffering that our Saviour endured.

As many were astonied at thee; his visage was so marred more than any man, and his form more than the sons of men. (Isaiah 52:14) The word **astonied** means to *stun or intransitively grow numb, devastate or stupefy, astonishment, amazed and confounded with fear.* Those who would see the Saviour in His suffering would be horrified at His appearance. He was repulsive to look upon. He was beaten, covered with blood and spit and did not even appear human. No wonder the Prophet says, **He hath no form nor comeliness; and when we shall see him, there is no beauty that we should desire him. (Isaiah 53:2)**

Isaiah says of Christ, **His visage was so marred more than any man, and his form more than the sons of men.** The word **visage** speaks of His *appearance.* The word **marred** means *to be disfigured.* The text continues **and his form more than the sons of men.** He no longer appeared to be human. Albert Barnes said, Jesus *was so disfigured as to retain scarcely the appearance of a man.*

This brutal disfiguring of the Christ was prophesied earlier by the Psalmist. **But I am a worm, and no man; a reproach of men, and despised of the people. (Psalm 22:6)** The word **worm** specifically speaks of the crimson crocus grub that when crushed, furnished the scarlet red color for the royal robes of kings. In order to produce the dye for these robes the lowly worm had to be crushed. Of course, after the crushing had taken place the worm was no longer recognizable as such. So it was with Christ on the Cross where He was crushed under the weight of our sin. It was there under the wrath of God that He shed His blood for the sins of mankind. It is that crimson flow that makes it possible for us to be clothed in kingly robes of righteousness. All Jesus ever did was good and He suffered and died for it. This is the example for God's people to follow. This is the mind that we are to arm ourselves with.

PURITY

Peter says, **for he that hath suffered in the flesh hath ceased from sin. That he no longer should live the rest of his time in the flesh to the lusts of men, but to the will of God. (1 Peter 4:1b-2)** What exactly did Peter mean when he said, **he that hath suffered in the flesh hath ceased from sin?** Some have actually said that suffering cleanses people from sin. We know that is not the case for it is the blood of Christ that cleanses us from sin. Others take this to mean that when a Christian sufferers like Christ and dies, he stops sinning. Newsflash! All who die stop sinning, not just those who suffer. I believe we can better understand what Peter means by looking at the next verse. **That he no longer should live the rest of his time in the flesh to the lusts of men, but to the will of God. (1 Peter 4:2)** There is a contrast here, Peter is talking about the way we used to live compared to the way we live now that we are saved. It is a contrast between the unsaved and the saved life. Peter tells us that ceasing from sin means that we are no longer going to spend the rest of this life in the flesh doing the lusts of men, but rather the will of God.

Peter lists several sins. **For the time past of our life may suffice us to have wrought the will of the Gentiles, when we walked in lasciviousness, lusts, excess of wine, revellings, banquetings, and abominable idolatries. (1 Peter 4:3)**

1) The word **lasciviousness** means *indecent and shameless behavior.* It carries the idea of living without restraint. It is living according to lustful desires. It speaks of the day in which we live. A day when men and women have no shame about their sin. There used to be a time when folks would try to hide their sin. Now they have no shame. Men and women shack up together instead of getting married. The sin of sodomy is everywhere. Men with men and women with women. These people live for sensual pleasure, flaunting their wickedness in open defiance of God's law.

2) Next, is **Lusts.** This word speaks of *unlawful desires.* We are clearly commanded to abstain from such lusts. **Dearly beloved, I beseech you as strangers and pilgrims, abstain from fleshly lusts, which war against the soul. (1 Peter 2:11)** Paul wrote, **But put ye on the Lord Jesus Christ, and make not provision for the flesh, to fulfil the lusts thereof. (Romans 13:14)**

3) **Excess of wine** speaks of drunkenness. The world calls it alcoholism. They always try to dress it up and make it more acceptable. They contend that it is not a sin, but a disease. It is not alcoholism, it is drunkenness. It is a sin

of volition. It is clear that alcohol is absolutely forbidden in the Christian life. America is saturated with this wickedness. The poison of strong drink has starved more children; wrecked more lives, destroyed more homes; ruined more young people; filled more graves; and sent more people to Hell than any other sin known to man! Strong drink is clearly off limits for the Christian. Only a fool would drink. **Wine is a mocker, strong drink is raging: and whosoever is deceived thereby is not wise. (Proverbs 20:1)**

4) **Revellings** comes from the same word from which we get the word *orgy* and carries the idea of *carousing and partying*. It speaks of drunken parties filled with sexual promiscuity. It is the party scene of the day. People love carousing. They love to go to the night clubs and parties. The word **revellings** is used only twice in the New Testament. In the other occurrence Paul lists the works of the flesh and concludes with **revellings, and such like: of the which I tell you before, as I have also told you in time past, that they which do such things shall not inherit the kingdom of God. (Galatians 5:21)**

5) The word **banquetings** carries the idea of a drinking match, a drunken bout. It is similar to the previous word. It speaks of a drinking party.

6) Last in this list is **abominable idolatries.** This speaks of the worship of idols. We think of idols as statues or false gods and that is true. However, it goes much further than that. An idol is anything that takes the place of God in your life. It could be your work, food, books, education,

possessions, television, or fashion. Your family can be an idol. Anything that squeezes God out is an idol. People idolize ball players, Hollywood stars, musicians, and other worldly people. Christian, what is taking God's place in your life? That is your idol! Martin Luther said, "*Whatever your heart clings to and confides in, that is really your God.*"

The point Peter is making is simple. This is the way the unsaved live. We expect such behavior from those who do not know Christ. But God's people have been regenerated. We are a new creature. **For they that are after the flesh do mind the things of the flesh; but they that are after the Spirit the things of the Spirit. For to be carnally minded is death; but to be spiritually minded is life and peace. Because the carnal mind is enmity against God: for it is not subject to the law of God, neither indeed can be. So then they that are in the flesh cannot please God. (Romans 8:5-8) As** God's people we have made a clean break from the old life—we ceased from the old sinful lifestyle.

Wherein they think it strange that ye run not with them to the same excess of riot, speaking evil of you. (1 Peter 4:4) When a person gets saved, his life changes. He stops doing the things he use to do and starts doing things he never did before. He starts reading his Bible. He stops his drinking and carousing and starts going to Church. He stops his immoral behavior. He stops worshipping self and begins to worship the Savior. Their repentance reflects their regeneration. John the Baptist said, **Bring forth therefore fruits meet for repentance. (Matthew 3:8)** John the Baptist was looking for something more than a one-two-three, pray-after-me, three points and a poem profession. He was looking for fruit. Fruit in the believer's life is important. In fact, it is the purpose of our salvation. Jesus said, **Ye have not chosen me, but I have chosen you, and ordained you, that ye should go and bring forth fruit, and that your fruit should remain: that whatsoever ye shall ask of the Father in my name, he may give it you. (John 15:16)**

Fruit is the outward demonstration that something real has happened in the heart. That is what salvation is all about. Jesus said, **Herein is my Father glorified, that ye bear much fruit; so shall ye be my disciples. (John 15:8)** A person cannot be saved without a change taking place in his life. It may be slow and it may be small, but it will be sure! Jesus, in the parable of the sower, taught this truth. **But he that received seed into the good ground is he that heareth the word, and understandeth it; which also beareth fruit, and bringeth forth, some an hundredfold, some sixty, some thirty. (Matthew 13:23)** Notice that those who get saved bear fruit, **some an hundredfold, some sixty, some thirty.** All of them bear fruit; it does not say some zero, or some not any. A changed life is proof that salvation has taken place. It is the outward demonstration that something real has happened in the heart. A person cannot be saved without a change taking place in his life.

When we make a break from the old sinful lifestyle, notice how **they** respond. Peter says, **they think it strange that ye run not with them.** The **they** are the old friends and acquaintances. The used to be friends now scoffers. They think it strange that we don't run with them anymore. Not only do they think we are strange, but Peter says **speaking**

evil of you. (1 Peter 4:4) You mark it down! When you get saved and live for God your old crowd won't have anything good to say about you. The word for **speaking evil** is "*blasphemeo*" literally means "*to blaspheme.*" It carries the idea of "*slandering or defaming someone by speaking evil of them.*" Christian, you can expect it. If you live for Christ the unsaved, even your old friends and family will think you are strange and many will blaspheme and even hate you.

> **If the world hate you, ye know that it hated me before it hated you. If ye were of the world, the world would love his own: but because ye are not of the world, but I have chosen you out of the world, therefore the world hateth you. (John 15:18-19)**

This is where many professing Christians fail. They are not willing to identify with Christ. Many allow their fear of man and their love for the world to keep them from standing for Christ. Every Christian must make a decision here. He will either live all out for Christ or he will serve the world. You cannot sit on the fence. There is no middle ground, no straddling the fence, and no compromise on this issue. Jesus made this fact clear. **He that is not with me is against me; and he that gathereth not with me scattereth abroad. (Matthew 12:30)** Moses could have enjoyed all the comforts of Egypt, but he chose to stay true to God.

> **By faith Moses, when he was come to years, refused to be called the son of Pharaoh's daughter; Choosing rather to suffer affliction with the people of God, than to enjoy the pleasures of sin for a season; Esteeming the reproach of Christ**

greater riches than the treasures in Egypt: for he had respect unto the recompence of the reward. (Hebrews 11:24-26)

May we never be ashamed of the fact that Christ is our Saviour. God help us to stand and not waver.

PERSPECTIVE

Who shall give account to him that is ready to judge the quick and the dead. (1 Peter 4:5) This verse points us to the Second Coming Of Christ. God's people aren't to live for the here and now. We are to be focused on the there and then. **Beloved, now are we the sons of God, and it doth not yet appear what we shall be: but we know that, when he shall appear, we shall be like him; for we shall see him as he is. And every man that hath this hope in him purifieth himself, even as he is pure. (1 John 3:2-3)** Every man that hath this hope! What hope? The return of Christ—the rapture! The Christian who is expecting the any moment return of Christ will be a committed Christian. The Christian's duty is to live at all times the way he would want his Saviour to find him living at the rapture. Jesus Christ asked the question, **...when the Son of man cometh, shall he find faith on the earth?. (Luke 18:8)** To live a holy life we must have the right perspective. The faithful Christian is living and watching for the return of his Saviour.

PROCLAMATION

For for this cause was the gospel preached also to them that are dead, that they might be judged according to men in the flesh, but live according to God in the spirit. (1

Peter 4:6) These are sobering words indeed. Peter says, **For, for this cause,** that is, because these people will have to stand before God some day and give account, for this reason the gospel was preached to them. Some day all unbelievers will stand before God in judgment. **It is appointed unto men once to die, but after this the judgment. (Hebrews 9:27)** What a serious responsibility we have to go out and proclaim the good news of the gospel to the lost. It is tragic that most Christians have no witness among the lost. Don't tell me that you believe in a place so awful as Hell and yet you won't win people to Christ. You would have to be the meanest devil that ever lived to believe in the horrors of Hell and not busy yourself with the business of trying to keep people out of that place. Lost men and women are going to have to stand before God some day. This is why we proclaim the gospel.

PRAYER

But the end of all things is at hand: be ye therefore sober, and watch unto prayer. (1 Peter 4:7) Paul said, **be ye therefore sober.** The word **sober** carries the idea of being *sober minded* and *clear headed.* We must be able to think clearly. To think according to the word of God. We must be a people with discernment. **But he that is spiritual judgeth all things, yet he himself is judged of no man. (1 Corinthians 2:15)**

Next, Paul says, **watch unto prayer.** We are helpless without prayer. Prayerlessness is one of the biggest hindrances to God's work. James said, **ye have not, because ye ask not. (James 4:2)** The exhortations to pray are many,

Paul wrote, **Praying always with all prayer and supplication in the Spirit. (Ephesians 6:18)** Again, **always** speaks of continual prayer. John R. Rice used to say, *"Every failure is a prayer failure."* Prayer moves the hand and heart of God. Robert Hall, a great preacher of the last century has well said, *"The prayer of faith is the only power in the universe to which the Great Jehovah yields. Prayer is the sovereign remedy."* Sam P. Jones said, *"No man was ever conquered on his knees in prayer to God."* Continual prayer is prevailing prayer. Prayer must be persistent. If there is one truth that the Bible teaches about prayer, it is this – continuance in prayer! The Apostle John said it this way. **And this is the confidence that we have in him, that, if we ask any thing according to his will, he heareth us: And if we know that he hear us, whatsoever we ask, we know that we have the petitions that we desired of him. (1 John 5:14-15)** The word **confidence** means boldness and carries the idea of **a boldness to speak freely.** Praise God! We can have boldness when we come before God in prayer. **Let us therefore come boldly unto the throne of grace, that we may obtain mercy, and find grace to help in time of need. (Hebrews 4:16)** We must understand that prayer is both a privilege and a command. Jesus said, **men ought always to pray, and not to faint. (Luke 18:1)** The always speaks of continual prayer. The word **faint** means to be weak or weary and carries the idea of being exhausted. Jesus put His finger on one of man's biggest prayer problems. One of the reasons for failure in the Christian life is trying to labor apart from prayer. Prayer makes God a partner in our work. Jesus said, **without me ye can do nothing. (John 15:5)** It is a sad day when the prayer meeting is the least attended service in the average Church. Many churches have done away with the midweek prayer meeting because of the lack of interest. The sports arenas are still full on Wednesday nights. The malls are still doing a good business on Wednesday nights. The restaurants are doing quite a business on Wednesday nights. What a sad state for a child of God to be sitting at home in front of the television, out at a restaurant, shopping or anything else when the Church doors are open. God's people must return to the prayer closet.

PRIORITY

And above all things have fervent charity among yourselves: for charity shall cover the multitude of sins. Use hospitality one to another without grudging. (1 Peter 4:8-9) Notice that Peter says, **And above all things.** Everything Peter has said is important and we must practice them if we are to live in the shadow of eternity. But what he is saying here is that there is something we must be extra careful about. He admonishes us **above all things have fervent charity among yourselves.** Notice it not simply charity, but **fervent charity. Fervent** comes from the word "*ektenes* "and speaks of "*stretching and straining.*" The word was used of a horse as he strained and stretched out his neck as he approached the finish line. It speaks of hard work and Peter is telling us to have that kind of love among ourselves. Paul said:

> **Though I speak with the tongues of men and of angels, and have not charity, I am become as sounding brass, or a tinkling cymbal. And though I**

> have the gift of prophecy, and understand all mysteries, and all knowledge; and though I have all faith, so that I could remove mountains, and have not charity, I am nothing. And though I bestow all my goods to feed the poor, and though I give my body to be burned, and have not charity, it profiteth me nothing. (1 Corinthians 13:1-3)

Paul stressed the point that no matter what else we may have, it is worthless if practiced apart from love. Someone has well said, *"People don't care how much you know until they know how much you care."*

As every man hath received the gift, even so minister the same one to another, as good stewards of the manifold grace of God. (1 Peter 4:10) We serve others by using our spiritual gifts. Notice that we are to be good stewards of our spiritual gifts. It is tragic that so many Church members are idle in God's work. I heard about the Pastor who said his Church was 100% willing when it came to work. 20 % were willing to do all the work and the 80% were willing to let them. Unfortunately, that is how most Churches operate. Statistics show that only about 20% of the people do most of the work while the other 80% seldom get involved. That means that the average Church is running at 20% efficiency. That is not very good. Think about it this way. If your car was operating at 20% efficiency you would not have made it to Church this morning. If your heart was operating at 20% efficiency, you be very sick and in need of some help. The same is true of a Church. A Church operating at 20% efficiency is sick and in need of help.

Just imagine the impact that a Church would have if it were operating at 100% efficiency. That is the way God designed the Church to function. The Bible says that when Jesus ascended back into Heaven that He **gave gifts unto men. (Ephesians 4:8)** We are told that those gifts were given to us, **For the perfecting of the saints, for the work of the ministry, for the edifying of the body of Christ. (Ephesians 4:12)** Not only did He give gifts, He gave gifts to every believer. **But the manifestation of the Spirit is given to every man to profit withal. (1 Corinthians 12:7)** No believer is without a gift and some believers have more than one gift. The Church was not designed to chug it way through the world firing hit and miss on a few cylinders. God's people were given gifts that the Church might operate at peak efficiency.

PRINCIPLE

If any man speak, let him speak as the oracles of God; if any man minister, let him do it as of the ability which God giveth: that God in all things may be glorified through Jesus Christ, to whom be praise and dominion for ever and ever. Amen. (1 Peter 4:11) The word **oracles** means "*spoken or uttered.*" Peter is saying, if you speak, then speak the Word of God. The need of the hour is for God's people to stay by the Word of God. There are many today who do not believe the Word of God. They tell us that there are mistakes in the Bible. Jesus said, **...O fools, and slow of heart to believe all that the prophets have spoken. (Luke 24:25)** Such people are identified by Christ as fools. In all the annals of time there has never been a book so precious and majestic as the King James Bible. The reason being, **For the prophecy came not in old time by the will of man: but holy men of God spake as they were moved by the holy Ghost. (2 Peter 1:21)** The Bible is a God-breathed book. The Bible contains the mind of God, the condition of man, and the clear, simple plan of salvation. The Lord Jesus Christ is the Wonderful and glorious theme of the Bible. His salvation shines forth from its pages as a guiding light to whoever desires to be saved. We are to speak according to God's word.

Next, **if any man minister, let him do it as of the ability which God giveth.** The work of God is not accomplished in our strength. There is too much self and too little Spirit in most of what we see these days. Jesus gave us the Holy Spirit to empower us to walk for and serve Him. **I send the promise of my Father upon you: but tarry ye in the city of Jerusalem, until ye be endued with power from on high. (Luke 24:49)** It is the Spirit of God that furnishes the power to live the Christian life. **Not by might, nor by power, but by my spirit, saith the LORD of hosts. (Zechariah 4:6)** Jesus said, **It is the spirit that quickeneth; the flesh profiteth nothing.... (John 6:63)** Nothing good can come from a flesh driven life.

Peter says, **that God in all things may be glorified through Jesus Christ, to whom be praise and dominion for ever and ever. Amen.** This is what it is all about! Bringing glory to God ought to be the only desire of the believer. We do not serve to exalt ourselves. We see a lot of this foolishness. There are far too many preachers looking for fame and fortune. They thrive on the applause of man. They are like Diotrephes **who loveth to have the preeminence. (John 1:9)** We live in a sad day when men stand and claim for themselves the glory that belongs to Jesus Christ. Next time you hear or read of one of these glory mongers bragging himself to high Heaven, remember the words of Jesus, **He that speaketh of himself seeketh his own glory. (John 7:18)** A true man of God will give Jesus Christ the glory. As God's people we need a revival of humility. Like John the Baptist our heart ought to be, **He must increase, but I must decrease. (John 3:30)** It is not about us. Let's get back to bragging on Jesus.

How To Survive Your Trials
1 Peter 4:12-19

The Bible teaches us that one of the main reason for a Christian being criticized and persecuted is his or her godly life. Peter has used Christ's suffering as an example of what we will face if we are faithful in living a holy life in this hostile world. Jesus also warned us of trouble in this world. He said:

> … **In the world ye shall have tribulation: but be of good cheer; I have overcome the world. (John 16:33)**

Here in this section Peter continues on the subject of suffering for Christ and he gets down to the nuts and bolts of survival.

EXPECT YOUR TRIALS

Beloved, think it not strange concerning the fiery trial which is to try you, as though some strange thing happened unto you. (1 Peter 4:12) Too often the gospel presented with the promise, "*Just trust Christ as Saviour and everything will be OK!*" That is simply not true. When one gets saved everything is OK as far as his salvation is concerned. It is a wonderful privilege to be saved and experience the salvation of the Lord. However, the saved soon finds out that living for Christ in this wicked world is not a peaches and cream deal. Anyone who is set on selling out to Christ and living whole heartedly for Him will soon find that he is running against the current. As a result there will be persecution and suffering. Peter gives us two thoughts here as he instructs us to expect trials.

The Counsel In The Trial

Beloved, think it not strange ... as though some strange thing happened unto you. Too often we hear Christian's whining because of difficulties in life. Why did this have to happen to me? I can't believe this happened to me! What a terrible testimony for the cause of Christ. We are so comfortable and spoiled today that even the slightest difficulty trips us up. Peter says, **think it not strange.** Don't think something unusual or strange has happened to you. Instead expect it to happen. J. Nieboer said:

> "Suffering is not a strange or alien thing to Christianity. First of all, Christ suffered much. Tradition tells us that all the apostles, excepting John, suffered martyrdom. Thousands of the early Christians were persecuted in every conceivable way, and as we look about us, we see many suffering today. It is not to be wondered at that it is so. Besides the testings of the Lord, we have heartless enemies. Satan is the God of this world. (II Cor. 4:4) and he will make it as hard for the Lord's people as he can. The world lies in the lap of the wicked one, and hates to be aroused from its sleep of death. They too, will do all in their power to hinder a Christian."

Jesus said, **But beware of men: for they will deliver you up to the councils, and they will scourge you in their synagogues; And ye shall be brought before governors and**

kings for my sake, for a testimony against them and the Gentiles ... The disciple is not above his master, nor the servant above his lord. (Matthew 10:17-18, 24) Don't think that it is an unusual thing when you are persecuted. It is not unusual it is to be expected. Jesus said, **If the world hate you, ye know that it hated me before it hated you. (John 15:18)** Paul, in the book of Hebrews names the great Hall of Faith heroes in chapter eleven. As we read about these men and women we note that they suffered much for their faith. They are described as those who **had trial of cruel mockings and scourgings, yea, moreover of bonds and imprisonment: They were stoned, they were sawn asunder, were tempted, were slain with the sword: they wandered about in sheepskins and goatskins; being destitute, afflicted, tormented;. (Of whom the world was not worthy:) they wandered in deserts, and in mountains, and in dens and caves of the earth. (Hebrews 11:36-38)** There will be trials in the Christian life. Just expect it.

The Cause Of The Trial

Next, Peter says, **the fiery trial which is to try you.** This is a plain statement. The trials that come into our life are for the purpose of trying us. Notice how Peter uses the word **fiery** to describe these trial. The word simply means burning and takes us back to the refining of Gold and Silver. Peter has already said, **That the trial of your faith, being much more precious than of gold that perisheth, though it be tried with fire. (1 Peter 1:7a)** Here we have the analogy of gold being refined by fire. For raw gold to be purified it must be melted and the dross skimmed off. God does the same thing with our faith. He allows our faith to enter into the fire. He allows these trials and afflictions into our lives for the purpose of burning off the impurities and leaving us with pure, genuine faith.

As the fining pot for silver, and the furnace for gold; so is a man to his praise. (Proverbs 27:21)

David said:

For thou, O God, hast proved us: thou hast tried us, as silver is tried. (Psalms 66:10)

A trial is the hand of God at work in your life. We simply need to accept trials as a normal part of the Christian life.

ENJOY YOUR TRIALS

But rejoice, inasmuch as ye are partakers of Christ's sufferings; that, when his glory shall be revealed, ye may be glad also with exceeding joy. If ye be reproached for the name of Christ, happy are ye; for the spirit of glory and of God resteth upon you: on their part he is evil spoken of, but on your part he is glorified. (1 Peter 4:13-14) The context is suffering and Peter uses such terms as **rejoice, be glad also with exceeding joy,** and **happy are ye.** These are terms that we wouldn't usually associate with suffering. However, Peter is teaching us that increased sufferings result in increased joy. We rejoice to the degree that we suffer. We are not accustomed to thinking this way, but the word of God teaches that there is joy in suffering for the cause of Christ. When the Apostles were persecuted, the Bible says:

And they departed from the presence of the council rejoicing that they were counted worthy to suffer shame for his name. (Acts 5:41)

When Paul and Silas were imprisoned for preaching Christ we are told that they **prayed and sang praises unto God: and the prisoners heard them. (Acts 16:25)** Paul also said, **But we glory in tribulations. (Romans 5:3)** The reason for our rejoicing is that we have a different perspective. We are not self-centered, we are Christ centered. The Christian life is not about us, it is about Him. Notice that the text says we are, **partakers of Christ's sufferings; that, when his glory shall be revealed, ye may be glad also with exceeding joy.** Notice that this is about revealing Christ's glory. The word **revealed** means to "*unveil, to uncover, to cause something to be known.*" Our suffering is designed to reveal Christ in our lives. If I handle suffering right, Christ is revealed to all those around me. **For I reckon that the sufferings of this present time are not worthy to be compared with the glory which shall be revealed in us. (Romans 8:18)**

EVALUATE YOUR TRIALS

The subject of Christian suffering is the theme of First Peter. We can suffer for good or evil. Whenever we are going through trials, we must stop and ask ourselves, Why am I going through this? That is we need to evaluate. Our suffering is not always for Christ's sake.

But let none of you suffer as a murderer, or as a thief, or as an evildoer... . (1 Peter 4:15a) A lot of folks are suffering because they break the laws of the land. They are simply suffering the consequences of their actions. When that happens, don't say, I am suffering for Christ. You are not. You are suffering because you broke the law.

Peter goes on to say, ... **or as a busybody in other men's matters. (1 Peter 4:15b)** Nothing will cause you more trouble than meddling in other people's affairs. This refers to those who can't keep their noses out of other people's business. Solomon said, **He that passeth by, and meddleth with strife belonging not to him, is like one that taketh a dog by the ears. (Proverbs 26:17)** To take a dog by the ears is sure to result in pain and suffering. To meddle with other people's problems is just as painful and will cause great problems.

Yet if any man suffer as a Christian, let him not be ashamed; but let him glorify God on this behalf. (1 Peter 4:16) It is shameful to suffer for foolish things like breaking the law or sticking our nose into someone else's business. But when we suffer as a Christian it is a different story. Peter said, **let him not be ashamed.** If you are suffering because you're a Christian, then you have nothing to be ashamed of. It is not disgraceful for a Christian to suffer for Christ. Instead Peter says, **but let him glorify God on this behalf.** Hold your head up high and give God the glory for what He is doing in your life.

For the time is come that judgment must begin at the house of God: and if it first begin at us, what shall the end be of them that obey not the gospel of God?. (1 Peter 4:17) These are sobering words and every child of God ought to take them seriously. One of the age old questions is Why do God's people suffer when unbelievers prosper? Why do

God's people seem to have so many problems when drunks, dopers, wife beaters and so forth seem to get by and enjoy life? Well, don't miss the fact that their judgment is coming. The text says, if we who are God's children are experiencing the judgment of God, **what shall the end be of them that obey not the gospel of God?**

When Peter says, **For the time is come that judgment must begin at the house of God,** he was speaking of the fact that trials and tribulations that his readers were already suffering, were allowed by God as His judgment. God often allows these tribulations and trials to come upon us to get our attention and correct us. The Great White Throne Judgment awaits the unbeliever—they will get theirs. However, the Christian does not escape the correcting hand of God also.

EXCEL IN YOUR TRIALS

Wherefore let them that suffer according to the will of God commit the keeping of their souls to him in well doing, as unto a faithful Creator. (1 Peter 4:19) Notice again that our suffering is **according to the will of God.** It is not because the enemy has the upper hand. Satan is not winning the battle in our lives just because we have problems. If we face these trials right—we win. These trials **according to the will of God** are for our good and His glory. That our trials are by His will means that He has planned and designed them. Everything that comes into our lives comes by divine design. If God wills suffering then so be it. It is better to suffer in the will of God than out of it. If God wills something for our lives then He will give us sustaining grace.

Peter tells us to commit the keeping of our souls to God. The word **commit** is from *"paratithemi "*which means *"to deposit for safekeeping."* This same word was used by Jesus on the cross when He said, **Father, into thy hands I commend my spirit. (Luke 23:46)** This reminds us that God is our keeper. Just as Jesus committed His soul to God for safekeeping, we are to entrust our souls to God for safekeeping as we face the trials of life. We are to survive our trials, not succumb to them.

The Pastoral Ministry
1 Peter 5:1-4

We now come to a new section of 1 Peter dealing with the issues of Pastoral leadership. The Pastor's work is no small matter. In fact, it is a momentous work. As a Pastor leads the local Church there are many duties and function that he must carry out.

THE REALITY OF PASTORAL WORK

The elders which are among you I exhort, who am also an elder, and a witness of the sufferings of Christ, and also a partaker of the glory that shall be revealed. (1 Peter 5:1) Peter could have taken the title Apostle, but instead he referred to himself as a fellow elder. Peter reminds us that he was a **witness of the sufferings of Christ.** Peter had seen the agony of Christ in Gethsemane. He had witnessed the mock trials and the beating of Christ as well as horrors of the crucifixion. He further states that he had also been **a partaker of the glory that shall be revealed.** Peter had witnessed the glorified Christ on the Mount of Transfiguration. He has seen Christ's face shine like the sun with the glory of God. Peter had seen Christ ascend back into Heaven in Acts chapter one. In addition to all that he had witnessed he had received the charge directly from Christ, **feed my sheep. (John 21:16-17)** When Peter speaks of Pastoral work he speaks with authority. He is well qualified to instruct us concerning the reality of the leadership.

Peter uses the term **elder** in referring to the pastorate. Some misunderstand the meaning of elder thinking it refers to the older men of the Church. While the term can refer to older men, the context here implies otherwise. When we find the term elder in reference to New Testament leadership it has nothing to do with chronological age. The term elder actually speaks of maturity. In First Timothy Paul gave Timothy the qualifications for an elder. **Not a novice, lest being lifted up with pride he fall into the condemnation of the devil. (1 Timothy 3:6)** A **novice** is a new convert—one who is unseasoned and untrained. So when we talk about an elder, we are not necessarily talking about somebody who is sixty or seventy years old. We are talking about someone who is experienced in the Christian faith, someone who has been saved a while and has a good working knowledge of the Bible as well as a good testimony.

THE RESPONSIBILITY OF PASTORAL WORK

Our English word *"pastor"* comes from the Latin and means *"shepherd."* The word Pastor well describes the heart of his ministry, that of shepherding the flock. Pastoring a church is tending to the Lord's flock. Pastoring is a work that is not only significant, but also carries with it a great deal of responsibility.

The Pastor is to Preach The Scriptures

Feed the flock of God which is among you.... (1 Peter 5:2a) This is a Divine charge. The command to **Preach the**

word. (2 Timothy 4:2) stands at the forefront when it comes to the Pastor's duties. We believe in the primacy of preaching—that preaching is supreme. As Paul left Ephesus he called the Pastors together and charged them to be faithful in their preaching.

> **But none of these things move me, neither count I my life dear unto myself, so that I might finish my course with joy, and the ministry, which I have received of the Lord Jesus, to testify the gospel of the grace of God. And now, behold, I know that ye all, among whom I have gone preaching the kingdom of God, shall see my face no more. Wherefore I take you to record this day, that I am pure from the blood of all men. For I have not shunned to declare unto you all the counsel of God. Take heed therefore unto yourselves, and to all the flock, over the which the Holy Ghost hath made you overseers, to feed the church of God, which he hath purchased with his own blood. (Acts 20:24-28)**

A faithful Pastor will declare the whole counsel of God. Paul was free from the blood of all men because he was faithful in preaching the Word of God. Churches and Christians are dying because they don't know how to live a faithful and Godly Christian life. The call is to preach and the content of preaching is the Word of God.

God's people are fed and equipped for service through the ministry of God's Word. **And he gave some, apostles; and some, prophets; and some, evangelists; and some, pastors and teachers; For the perfecting of the saints, for the work of the ministry, for the edifying of the body of Christ.**

(Ephesians 4:11-12) Peter uses the analogy of shepherding to illustrate his point. The Shepherd must see to it that the sheep are fed. Left to themselves sheep do not eat well. They will graze in poor pasture and eat things that are not good for them. Since sheep cannot discern between nourishing plants and those that are poison, they will eat poisonous plants that will do them much harm and possibly even kill them if they are not cared for and watched over by the shepherd. When sheep are not fed or when they are fed the wrong diet they will not be satisfied.

The reason we see so many hurting and wayward Christians in this world is because they are not being fed properly. When preaching is neglected, the people of God will suffer. No shepherd will have a healthy flock unless he feeds them appropriately. The Pastor must take his responsibility seriously and warn of behavior that is not pleasing and honoring to God. Matthew Henry said:

> "Do this work with all fervency of spirit. Call upon those under [your] charge to take heed of sin, to do their duty: call upon them to repent, and believe, and live a holy life and this both in season and out of season … We must do it in season, that is, let slip no opportunity; and do it out of season, that is, not shift off the duty, under pretence that it is out of season"

This is a good time to point out that the shepherd must be well-informed and knowledgeable about the vegetation. He must have a good working knowledge about what is good for their health and what is not good or hazardous. He must be able to feed his flock the right things and keep them away from the wrong things.

The Pastor is to Preside Over The Saints

The Pastor's responsibilities includes **taking the oversight thereof. (1 Peter 5:2b)** The shepherd is much more than a preacher who simply fills the pulpit. He is the Chief Shepherd's under-shepherd—he is the leader of the local Church where God has placed him. Peter speaks of the Pastor as **taking the oversight.** He leads the Church as Christ leads him. The modern Church has turned it around and the Pastors is led by the board. This is why so many Churches have died. The Scriptures clearly teach believers to **Obey them that have the rule over you, and submit yourselves: for they watch for your souls, as they that must give account, that they may do it with joy, and not with grief: for that is unprofitable for you. (Hebrews 13:17)** The Pastor of the local church is responsible for the people of that Church and will give account to Jesus Christ, the **chief Shepherd,** for every Christian under his leadership.

The Pastor is to Promote The Saviour

Under-shepherds are to **feed the flock of God** Whose flock? God's! Too many pastors in our day are promoting themselves rather that the **chief Shepherd.** Pastors must remember that they have been given responsibility for tending a flock that belongs to God, not to themselves. Notice the statement **and when the chief Shepherd shall appear**. It is all about Jesus, the Chief Shepherd. A Pastor must lift up Jesus Christ and Him alone before his flock.

Many leaders have their people looking at them, rather than their Saviour. It is Christ who came nearly two thousand years ago to die on Calvary's cross for their sin, and it is He who will return for them.

THE REQUIREMENTS OF PASTORAL WORK

Peter lays out some requirements for the manner in which the Pastor is to lead the local Church.

The Right Desire

Peter says, **not by constraint, but willingly ... but of a ready mind. (1 Peter 5:2b)** This speaks of the Pastor's heart to serve. Too often Pastors get caught up in a woe is me mentality. They say, *"Why am I bothering with this Church. No one cares about me, I have to do everything by myself. If I don't do it no one else will. People just don't understand how hard my field is. My people just don't appreciate me."* What a sad outlook on the ministry! I have seen a lot of preachers wash out because of such an attitude. The fact of the matter is, we are called of God into the greatest work in the world. It doesn't matter who acknowledges our work. It doesn't matter who praises us so long as God is pleased with us. The Pastor does not serve because he has to, but willingly. He doesn't serve because he can't find better work. To the Pastor there is no better work than God's work. He serves with joy because that's what God wants.

The Right Drive

The Pastor does not serve for **filthy lucre. (1 Peter 5:2c)** The Pastor is not in it for the money. The phrase **filthy lucre** carries the idea of *shameful gain.* It is shameful to be in the ministry for the money. The call of the Pastor is not a vocational call. If a Pastor develops the wrong attitude about money he will become a hireling rather than a shepherd. A man who cares more about his paycheck than he does about the sheep should probably find a different line of work. Jeremiah said:

> **For from the least of them even unto the greatest of them every one is given to covetousness; and from the prophet even unto the priest every one dealeth falsely. (Jeremiah 6:13)**

Jesus spoke about the difference between a shepherd and a hireling:

> **I am the good shepherd: the good shepherd giveth his life for the sheep. But he that is an hireling, and not the shepherd, whose own the sheep are not, seeth the wolf coming, and leaveth the sheep, and fleeth: and the wolf catcheth them, and scattereth the sheep. The hireling fleeth, because he is an hireling, and careth not for the sheep. (John 10:11-13)**

A man that is in the ministry for the paycheck will fail to serve the sheep. That being said, let's at the same time be aware of the fact that it is not wrong for Pastors to desire enough money to take care of their family and pay their bills. God intends for His people to take good care of the Pastor. Paul said, **Even so hath the Lord ordained that they which preach the gospel should live of the gospel. (1 Corinthians 9:14)** Supporting a preacher is God's ordained means of caring for His workers. Paul said, **Let the elders that rule** well be counted worthy of double honour, especially they who labour in the word and doctrine. For the scripture saith, Thou shalt not muzzle the ox that treadeth out the corn. And, The labourer is worthy of his reward. (1 Timothy 5:17-18)** A church that wants to please God must see to it that their pastor is properly cared for—that his needs are met, that they have enough money to pay their bills, and that they are not financially hindered because they're in the ministry.

The Right Demeanor

Neither as being lords over God's heritage. (1 Peter 5:3a) That the Pastor has authority cannot be disputed, but the Pastor must remember that his is a delegated authority. This word translated **lord** carries the idea of forcefully ruling over something or of being domineering. The word was used of bringing something into subjection by force. This verse warns against the Pastor becoming power hungry. A Pastor taking the oversight and exercising his God-given authority is not wrong, but lording over God's heritage is. The Pastor will accomplish nothing by strong arming the flock.

The Right Demonstration

Peter says, **but being ensamples to the flock. (1 Peter 5:3b)** The best way to lead is by example. Paul led by example. **Not because we have not power, but to make ourselves an ensample unto you to follow us. (2 Thessalonians 3:9)** Paul did not operate solely by his power and authority—he was an example for others. Later, Paul would instruct a young preacher by the name of Timothy to

be thou an example of the believers, in word, in conversation, in charity, in spirit, in faith, in purity. (1 Timothy 4:12) This is leading as opposed to lording. Shepherds go before their sheep to lead them. You will never see a shepherd driving the sheep in front of him. Pastors must lead the people of God along the paths of life feeding and caring for them.

THE REWARD OF PASTORAL WORK

And when the chief Shepherd shall appear, ye shall receive a crown of glory that fadeth not away. (1 Peter 5:4) Peter reminds us that Jesus is the chief Shepherd and that He is coming back. When He returns every Pastor will answer to Him. We will stand before Him and give an account for our work. Paul commanded believers **to Obey them that have the rule over you, and submit yourselves.... (Hebrews 13:17a)** To obey and submit is the believer's responsibility. But notice the Pastor's accountability. In the same verse Paul says, **for they watch for your souls, as they that must give account, that they may do it with joy, and not with grief: for that is unprofitable for you. (Hebrews 13:17b)** The Pastor will answer to the Lord for his leadership. Likewise the believer will answer to the Lord for his followship.

The Pastor who has done well will receive a **crown of glory.** The filthy lucre, the power, everything that sidetracks the preacher in the here and now is just temporary. But notice that the preacher who stays by the stuff and serves his people will receive a reward **that fadeth not away.** What a solemn responsibility—to pastor God's people!

A young pastor of a small church complained to Charles H. Spurgeon about the smallness of his church with so few members. Spurgeon asked him, How many members do you have?

Fifty, said the young pastor.

Ah, exclaimed Spurgeon, that's more than you will want to account for on the Day of Judgment.

The crown of glory will be awarded only to those under-shepherds who have been faithful in carrying out their duties. What a responsibility! Faithful shepherds who are often dishonored and ridiculed on earth will in Heaven receive a crown of glory from Christ, the chief Shepherd Whom they followed and served.

Getting Ahead In The Christian Life
1 Peter 5:5-7

There are two different groups in the opening verses of chapter 5. There are the **elders. (5:1)** speaking of the Pastors of the local churches and there are the **younger. (5:5)** of the congregation. These people to whom Peter was writing must have had a problem with submission. Peter had already admonished them to submit to government. (1 Peter 2:13-14), to their employers. (1 Peter 2:18), wives to their husbands. (1 Peter 3:1) and now Church members to their Pastors.

PLACE TO OCCUPY

Likewise, ye younger, submit yourselves unto the elder. Yea, all of you be subject one to another.... (1 Peter 5:5a) The word **likewise** tells us that same subject is under discussion. The discussion of the first four verses focused on the office of the Pastor and his responsibility while these verses focus on the congregation and their responsibility. Peter says, **submit yourselves unto the elder.** This word **submit** is always used in the Bible of submission to a person who has a recognized office of authority such as a parent, an employer, or a government leader. The commandment here is for the congregation to submit to the leadership of their Pastor. Not many folks like submission. Most would rather be in authority. However, not everyone can be in charge. We hear a lot of talk about leadership, but leadership without fellowship goes nowhere. Peter addresses the rank and file

Christians and makes the point that a congregation cannot function properly without a recognition of authority. **And we beseech you, brethren, to know them which labour among you, and are over you in the Lord, and admonish you. (1 Thessalonians 5:12)**

PRINCIPLE TO OBEY

Peter went on to say, **and be clothed with humility: for God resisteth the proud, and giveth grace to the humble. (1 Peter 5:5b)** Now Peter deals with the number one thing that hinders submission—that is pride. Pride will ruin you. Remember! Pride is what turned a beautiful angel into the devil. Of the things that God hates, **a proud look** is at the top of the list. (Proverbs 6:17) Solomon said:

> **When pride cometh, then cometh shame. (Proverbs 11:2)**
>
> **The LORD will destroy the house of the proud.... (Proverbs 15:25)**
>
> **Every one that is proud in heart is an abomination to the LORD: though hand join in hand, he shall not be unpunished. (Proverbs 16:5)**
>
> **A man's pride shall bring him low.... (Proverbs 29:23)**

There is no future in pride. The prideful man is dangerous because he has no fear of God, **The fear of the LORD is to hate evil: pride, and arrogancy .... (Proverbs 8:13)** Prideful people are hard to work with because they won't listen. They are bull-headed and their pride won't let them submit to leadership. There are a lot Christians sitting in Churches with the attitude that *"no preacher is going to tell me what to do!"* Such people should remember that when they buck against God-ordained authority they are bucking against God. It is God Who ordained the authority. No organization can function without authority.

Instead of pride, we are to **be clothed with humility.** Peter uses the metaphor of clothing ourselves to show us the importance of humility. Clothing is usually the first thing you notice when you see someone. There are books available on How To Dress For Success. How you dress is important. Just as clothes cover the body, so the believer should be literally covered with humility. Humility is an attitude that puts others first. Submission is not a problem to one who is clothed in humility. A humble person will have no problem submitting to authority. Paul said, **Let nothing be done through strife or vainglory; but in lowliness of mind let each esteem other better than themselves. Look not every man on his own things, but every man also on the things of others. (Philippians 2:3-4)**

Peter says that **God resisteth the proud.** The word **resisteth** means *"to set against, to stand against."* It is a military term that describes resisting an enemy army. The idea here is that God is set against proud people who do not submit to authority in the local Church. God resists those who resist authority.

Humble yourselves therefore under the mighty hand of God. (1 Peter 5:6a) Notice that this humbling comes **under the mighty hand of God.** It is not the preacher that is trying to get you to submit—it is God Who wants you to submit. You are not just fighting the Pastor, you're fighting God. The

Bible says, **Woe unto him that striveth with his Maker!. (Isaiah 45:9a)**

Peter says, **that he may exalt you in due time. (1 Peter 5:6b)** The word **exalt** means "*to be lifted up.*" Man tries to lift himself up in pride, but God rejects it. The only way for man to be truly lifted up is to humble himself and let God lift him. Jesus said, **For whosoever exalteth himself shall be abased; and he that humbleth himself shall be exalted. (Luke 14:11)** This exaltation comes **in due time.** Not in our time, but in God's time.

THE PRACTICE TO OBSERVE

Casting all your care upon him; for he careth for you. (1 Peter 5:7) Note that the word casting is in the present tense connecting it with the previous verse. Don't miss this! Peter is not changing direction here. He is continuing with the same thought. In verse six we are commanded to humble ourselves and in verse seven he tells us how to humble ourselves. We attain humility by casting all our care upon the Lord. The main thing that hinders our humility is the take care of old number one mentality. If I don't take care of myself who will? Prideful people are always exalting themselves, they are trying to lift themselves up while humble people are lifted up by God. The idea here is just stop worrying about all of that and give it to God. He will take care of it because He **careth for you.** The Psalmist said, **Cast thy burden upon the LORD, and he shall sustain thee: he shall never suffer the righteous to be moved. (Psalms 55:22)**

You Better Be Careful Out There
1 Peter 5:8-14

Satan and his forces are set on hindering the work and will of God. Paul experienced it, many other Bible men and women experienced it, and so will we. We are warned to, **Be sober, be vigilant; because your adversary the devil, as a roaring lion, walketh about, seeking whom he may devour. (1 Peter 5:8)** We better be careful out there.

A SOBERING WATCH

Be sober, be vigilant. (1 Peter 5:8a) Peter starts this section with a two-fold command. This is where victory over Satan begins.

First, we are to **be sober.** The word **sober** means to be *discreet and cautious* and carries the idea of being *discerning.* The Christian must develop discernment! Without discernment the child of God will become food for the lion. Paul said, **But the natural man receiveth not the things of the Spirit of God: for they are foolishness unto him: neither can he know them, because they are spiritually discerned. But he that is spiritual judgeth all things, yet he himself is judged of no man. For who hath known the mind of the Lord, that he may instruct him? But we have the mind of Christ. (1 Corinthians 2:14-16)** Noah Webster defines discernment as:

> "The act of discerning; also, the power or faculty of the mind, by which it distinguishes one thing from another, as truth from falsehood, virtue from

vice; acuteness of judgment; power of perceiving differences of things or ideas, and their relations and tendencies."

The sobriety Peter is talking about is the ability to see things in their true light. The word **sober** paints a vivid picture. A drunken person is not sober. He neither has clear thinking nor control over himself. Solomon aptly describe a person under the influence of alcohol.

> **Who hath woe? who hath sorrow? who hath contentions? who hath babbling? who hath wounds without cause? who hath redness of eyes? They that tarry long at the wine; they that go to seek mixed wine. Look not thou upon the wine when it is red, when it giveth his colour in the cup, *when* it moveth itself aright. At the last it biteth like a serpent, and stingeth like an adder. Thine eyes shall behold strange women, and thine heart shall utter perverse things. Yea, thou shalt be as he that lieth down in the midst of the sea, or as he that lieth upon the top of a mast. They have stricken me, shalt thou say, and I was not sick; they have beaten me, and I felt it not: when shall I awake? I will seek it yet again. (Proverbs 23:29-35)**

Drunk people do dumb things because their thinking is impaired. They have a lack of discernment. There are a lot of professing Christians who are not spiritually sober. They do not see things in their true light. They are easily swayed by slick words and appearances. Believers are not to be drunk, but sober, alert and discerning.

Second, we are to **be vigilant.** The word **vigilant** means to *be alert, awake and on the lookout.* We are to be on the lookout and actually watching for Satanic attack. The call to be vigilant and watch is a common one in Scripture.

> **Watch ye, stand fast in the faith, quit you like men, be strong. (1 Corinthians 16:13)**
>
> **Therefore let us not sleep, as *do* others; but let us watch and be sober. (1 Thessalonians 5:6)**
>
> **Continue in prayer, and watch in the same with thanksgiving. (Colossians 4:2)**

The word from which vigilant comes is very interesting. The Greeks used this word to describe the careful crossing of a river by stepping from one slippery stone to another. The word was also a military term meaning to stand guard. No wonder Jesus said, **And what I say unto you I say unto all, Watch. (Mark 13:37)**

A STERN WARNING

Peter says, **because your adversary the devil, as a roaring lion, walketh about, seeking whom he may devour. (1 Peter 5:8b)** This is a graphic picture that conveys the Prowl, Persistence and the Pride of Satan.

We see Satan's Prowl

Peter said that Satan **as a roaring lion, walketh about, seeking whom he may devour.** The picture is of a lion on the prowl. He is hungry, relentless and vicious. The lion moves with swiftness, silence and great strength. He is dangerous. He will stop at nothing to capture, rip apart and devour his prey.

We see Satan's Persistence

Notice that **walketh about** is in the present tense. Satan is always on the prowl. He does not let up. Satan is not asleep, he is not on vacation, he is not taking a break. Like a lion stalking a lamb, Satan is constantly looking for an opportunity to move in and devour his prey.

We see Satan's Pride

Satan is pictured here as a **roaring lion.** A lion never roars while it is prowling. The roar would warn the prey. The fact that he is **roaring** implies that Satan considers himself to have already conquered his prey. The roar of the lion does three things. **1)** The sudden roar terrorizes the prey just long enough to give Satan the edge. **2)** The roar is boast of triumph in which the king of the jungle announces his victory. **3)** The roar is a warning to the other animals to stay away while he enjoys his kill.

Satan's character is seen in his titles and names. A few of his names found in the Bible are: Abaddon. (Revelation 9:11); Accuser of our brethren. (Revelation 12:10); Adversary. (I Peter 5:8); Angel of the bottomless pit. (Revelation 9:11); Appollyon. (Revelation 9:11); Beelzebub. (Matthew 12:24); Belial. (2 Corinthians 6:15); the devil. (Matthew 4:1); Enemy. (Matthew 13:39); Evil spirit. (1 Sam. 16:14); Father of lies. (John 8:44); Liar. (John 8:44); Lying spirit. (I Kings 22:22); Murderer. (John 8:44); Old serpent. (Revelation 12:9); Power of darkness. (Colossians 1:13); Prince of devils. (Matthew 12:24); Ruler of darkness of this world. (Eph. 6:12); Serpent. (2 Corinthians 11:3); The spirit that now worketh in the children of disobedience. (Ephesians 2:2); Tempter. (Matthew 4:3); Unclean spirit. (Matthew 12:43); Wicked one. (Matthew 13:19, 38) The name **Satan** means *opponent* or *adversary* and is used over fifty times in the Bible. The name **Devil** means *slanderer* or *accuser* and it is also used over fifty times in the Word of God. His names alone reveal what he really is. He is a vicious and ferocious enemy. We better be careful out there.

A SERIOUS WARFARE

Whom resist stedfast in the faith, knowing that the same afflictions are accomplished in your brethren that are in the world. (1 Peter 5:9) Here we are commanded to resist our enemy. The word resist is a military term that speaks of an all out determination to defeat the opposition. War is a life or death situation. You don't play around when you are in battle. Believers get into trouble when they don't take the battle seriously. James gives us a good idea of what it means to resist the enemy. **Submit yourselves therefore to God. Resist the devil, and he will flee from you. (James 4:7)**

Peter goes on to say that we accomplish this by being, **stedfast in the faith. Stedfast** is also a military word. It means to be fixed and firm. It carries the idea of putting up a solid defense. We are to be fixed and firm in our faith.

A SURE WIN

But the God of all grace, who hath called us unto his eternal glory by Christ Jesus, after that ye have suffered a while.... (1 Peter 5:10a) Think about those words! **The God of all grace.** We may have a relentless and vicious enemy, but we have a gracious God! This is a precious promise. The suffering and the hurt doesn't last forever. It lasts only **a while.** Peter said, **after that ye have suffered.** This tells us that there is an end to misery and heartache that often plagues us in this world. The war won't last forever. There are better days ahead. Notice the contrast with God's **eternal glory.** Our suffering is only for **a while,** but our life with God is eternal.

Peter says that will **make you perfect, stablish, strengthen, settle you. (1 Peter 5:10b)** This is God's promise that He is not finished with us. Notice God's four-fold promise to the suffering believer.

First, God promises to make us **perfect**. The word **perfect** has to do with completion. It carries the idea of being completely furnished and whole. Satan can hinder us, but he cannot stop us. Paul said, **Being confident of this very thing, that he which hath begun a good work in you will perform it until the day of Jesus Christ. (Philippians 1:6)** Satan's aim is to destroy and devour us, but God's aim is to complete us.

Second, God promises to **stablish** us. The word **stablish** means to be steadfast, firm, and solid. It carries the idea of being immovable. Paul spoke of being **Rooted and built up in him, and stablished in the faith…. (Colossians 2:7)** It is the Lord Who stablishes us. **But the Lord is faithful, who shall stablish you, and keep you from evil. (2 Thessalonians 3:3)**

Third, God promises to **strengthen** us. The word simply means to be filled with strength. We are so weak and so powerless to live the Christian life. Man cannot do it by himself. **Not by might, nor by power, but by my spirit, saith the LORD of hosts. (Zechariah 4:6)** We can't, but God can. He will sufficiently strengthen us. No wonder Paul said, **I can do all things through Christ which strengtheneth me. (Philippians 4:13)**

Fourth, God promises to **settle** us. The word settle carries the idea of resting on a solid foundation. Paul said, **For other foundation can no man lay than that is laid, which is Jesus Christ. (1 Corinthians 3:11)** The foundation is always the least noticed, but the most important part of any building. If the foundation is not right the building will not stand. If you build your life and hope on anything less than Christ you will be disappointed.

A SATISFYING WORSHIP

To him be glory and dominion for ever and ever. Amen. (1 Peter 5:11) Peter breaks out in praise for God. Peter reminds us that God is the One Who has **glory and dominion** and that He has it **for ever and ever.** Here is the key to victory. No matter what we are facing, God is always good. No matter how dire the situation, it is temporal, but our relationship with God is eternal. The word **dominion** speaks of power and domination. Peter uses this word to remind us that we serve a Sovereign God. He is all powerful—everyone and everything is under His control. **The LORD hath prepared his throne in the heavens; and his kingdom ruleth over all. (Psalms 103:19)** Too many believers fail in trials because their worship life isn't right. Instead of worshiping and relying on God, they focus on the trial and become defeated. Always remember that God is in control. God is too good to be unkind, too wise to make mistakes and too powerful to be defeated. Yes! This life is a battlefield for the believer. We are engaged in a great warfare, but we are also involved in a great worship. He has all wisdom and all power and He is worthy of our praise. **To him be glory and dominion for ever and ever. Amen.**

SECOND PETER

How To Have A Fall Proof Life
2 Peter 1:5-11

Here Peter gives us some instruction on how to be a victorious and fruitful Christian.

A COMMAND TO ADD

And beside this, giving all diligence, add to your faith ... (2 Peter 1:5a) The phrase **giving all diligence** comes from *"pareisphero spoude"* and means *"to bear along side of and bring into."* The word **diligence** conveys the idea of *"intense effort coupled with haste, speed, eagerness, earnestness."* We are to make every effort to do what God requires. What has He required? That we eagerly and earnestly bring along side and into our lives the seven virtues that follow.

We Are To Add Virtue

Peter says, **add to your faith virtue... (2 Peter 1:5b) Virtue** speaks of *"moral excellence."* The Bible says of Stephen, **For he was a good man, and full of the Holy Ghost and of faith: and much people was added unto the Lord. (Acts 11:24)** The word actually carries the idea of *having moral strength and moral courage.* Joseph is a good example. When he was propositioned by Potiphar's wife the Bible says, **"he refused..." (Genesis 39:8a)** Without hesitation Joseph said *"no"* to his temptress. Joseph had the good character to make the right decision and said no to sin. Joseph stayed pure because he made a choice to stay pure.

We Are To Add Knowledge

... and to virtue knowledge; (2 Peter 1:5c) Renn says that **knowledge** is the, *"understanding and appreciation of the spiritual truths of the Christian faith."* We are to appreciate the word of God and study it, thereby acquiring practical knowledge that enables us to see situations from God's perspective and respond accordingly. Without such knowledge faith goes nowhere. We must learn God's word in order to be able to apply His principles to our life. God has promised to guide us. **I will instruct thee and teach thee in the way which thou shalt go: I will guide thee with mine eye. (Psalms 32:8)** That guidance come from the word of God. Jesus said, **Ye do err, not knowing the scriptures... (Matthew 22:29)** The Apostle Paul said under inspiration of the Holy Spirit, **So then faith cometh by hearing, and hearing by the word of God. (Romans 10:17)** It is through the Word of God that the believer is taught and corrected. **Now ye are clean through the word which I have spoken unto you. (John 15:3)** The only way to be fruitful in our Christian walk is to live a life based upon God's Word.

We Are To Add Temperance

And to knowledge temperance ... (2 Peter 1:6a) The word **temperance** speaks of *"self-control."* It carries the idea of being controlled and restrained. It means that our desires are under the control of the Holy Spirit. We are commanded to be **filled with the Spirit; Ephesians 5:18** The idea here is control. When He fills us He controls us. We will never overcome fleshly desires without Him. We must yield ourselves to the Spirit instead of the flesh. He then takes over and controls us.

We Are To Add Patience

... and to temperance patience ... (2 Peter 1:6b) Here is a tough one! The word **patience** comes from the Greek *"hypomone"* meaning to *"remain under."* It carries the idea of *"perseverance, endurance, fortitude, persistence regardless of the circumstances."* Patience is akin to **longsuffering** which is listed among the fruit of the Spirit. James said, **Blessed is the man that endureth temptation: for when he is tried, he shall receive the crown of life, which the Lord hath promised to them that love him. (James 1:12)** We must resolve to stay by the stuff no matter what others are doing.

We Are To Add Godliness

... and to patience godliness; (2 Peter 1:6c) Godliness is a general term that speaks of holy living. It means to be God-like. The idea is that of reflecting the traits of our heavenly Father. In his first letter Peter said, **But as he which hath called you is holy, so be ye holy in all manner of conversation. Because it is written, Be ye holy; for I am holy. (1 Peter 1:15-16)** God takes our holiness seriously. **Having therefore these promises, dearly beloved, let us cleanse ourselves from all filthiness of the flesh and spirit, perfecting holiness in the fear of God. (2 Corinthians 7:1)** We are to perfect holiness in our lives. The word **perfecting** speaks of *"finishing," "completing,"* or *"fulfilling."* It carries the idea of bringing something to its ultimate conclusion. God's people are to be an holy people. Later in this letter Peter says, **Seeing then that all these things shall be**

dissolved, what manner of persons ought ye to be in all holy conversation and godliness. (2 Peter 3:11)** God still demands holiness and therefore holiness must be a priority in the life of every believer. **Follow peace with all men, and holiness, without which no man shall see the Lord. Hebrews 12:14** Godliness means that we live our life the way Christ lived when He was on earth.

We Are To Add Kindness

And to godliness brotherly kindness... (2 Peter 1:7a) The word **kindness** come from the word *"philadelphia"* and speaks of brotherly love and affection. It is the a special love that exists between brothers and sisters within a loving family. This is the kind of affection we are to have for one another. It is a family love. **As we have therefore opportunity, let us do good unto all men, especially unto them who are of the household of faith. (Galatians 6:10)** It is the kind of love that Peter called the ... **unfeigned love of the brethren** and commanded us to **see that ye love one another with a pure heart fervently: (1 Peter 1:22)**

We Are To Add Charity

... and to brotherly kindness charity. (2 Peter 1:7b) The word charity comes from *"agape."* It is Calvary love. This a self-sacrificing love—a love that gives itself for the person loved. It is the kind of love that demands something of us. The supreme measure and example of *agape* love is God's love for sinners. **For God so loved the world, that he gave his only begotten Son, that whosoever believeth in him should not perish, but have everlasting life. (John 3:16)** The greatest demonstration of love this world has ever known is the cross of Calvary. The evidence of His unwavering love is the sacrifice of His Son for the sin of a lost world. **But God commendeth his love toward us, in that, while we were yet sinners, Christ died for us. (Romans 5:8)** This is the kind of love that knows no boundaries. It is sacrificial to the end. It is not seeking, it is giving. It is a love that is never selfish, self-serving, and self-seeking.

A CRISIS TO AVOID

For if these things be in you, and abound, they make you that ye shall neither be barren nor unfruitful in the knowledge of our Lord Jesus Christ. But he that lacketh these things is blind, and cannot see afar off, and hath forgotten that he was purged from his old sins. (2 Peter 1:8-9) Peter speaks of two tragic conditions that we must avoid.

We Must Avoid Barrenness

For if these things be in you, and abound, they make you that ye shall neither be barren nor unfruitful in the knowledge of our Lord Jesus Christ. (2 Peter 1:8) We must avoid the crisis of being **barren** and **unfruitful**. Fruit is the purpose of our existence. **Ye have not chosen me, but I have chosen you, and ordained you, that ye should go and bring forth fruit … (John 15:16)** In John 15 Jesus deals with the subject of fruit bearing. He speaks of **fruit, more fruit, much fruit,** and **fruit that remains!** The duty of the Christian is to bear fruit. Peter speaks, **unfruitful in the knowledge of our Lord Jesus Christ.** The idea is that if we apply the previous seven virtues to the foundation of our faith, we will know the Lord better. The better we know the Lord, the greater our relationship with Him and therefore, the greater our fruit bearing. So then, we want to avoid the crisis of being **barren** and **unfruitful.**

We Must Avoid Blindness

But he that lacketh these things is blind, and cannot see afar off, and hath forgotten that he was purged from his old sins. 2 Peter 1:9 There are dire consequences to those who lack **these things.** A person who does not have the seven spiritual virtues listed in verses 5-7 is spiritually blind. The phrase **cannot see afar off** is an interesting one. It comes from "*myōpazō.*" It is the word from which myopia is derived. Myopia is a medical term that speaks of being near-sighted. In the context this term means to be extremely limited in spiritual understanding and discernment. Those who fail to add to their faith are like near-sighted people who can see only that which is right in front of them. Spiritually near-sighted people see only the temporal. Because they fail to add to their faith they do not have the ability to discern spiritual things.

Solomon spoke of discernment as the ability ... **to perceive the words of understanding; Proverbs 1:2** The word **perceive** means *"to know, to separate or distinguish."* It is the ability to separate the facts from the false. Someone has referred to it as sanctified common sense. This is the ability to grasp or to get a hold on truth. Some folks are never able to get a hold on truth. **But the natural man receiveth not the things of the Spirit of God: for they are foolishness unto him: neither can he know them, because they are spiritually discerned. But he that is spiritual judgeth all things, yet he himself is judged of no man. For who hath known the mind of the Lord, that he may** instruct him? But we have the mind of Christ. (1 Corinthians 2:14-16)** The natural man, that is the unsaved man cannot get a good grasp on spiritual truth because it is spiritually discerned and he does not have the Spirit of God. He can understand the natural, but he cannot understand the supernatural. However, the big problem we are facing today is that so many professing Christians seem to have no grasp on truth. They are spiritually near-sighted because they have not added to their faith.

A CALL TO AFFIRM

Wherefore the rather, brethren, give diligence to make your calling and election sure … (2 Peter 1:10a) This is the second time Peter calls his readers to diligence. He is calling on us to make every effort to live for Christ. We are to move beyond profession to proof. It is easy to talk about being saved, but here we are called upon to live our Christianity. We are to give evidence of our salvation by holy and consecrated living.

A CONQUEST TO ACHIEVE

Peter says, **… for if ye do these things, ye shall never fall: 2 Peter 1:10b** Here is the secret to the victorious Christian life. **IF YE DO THESE THINGS!** If we are going to be victorious we are going to have to DO some things. Don't misunderstand me here! I know that salvation is entirely by grace. It is the free gift from God and our works can in no way add to it. However, salvation is more than being saved. Much of our Christian life is based upon doing. **Wherefore, my beloved, as ye have always obeyed, not as in my presence only, but now much more in my absence, work out your own salvation with fear and trembling.**

(Philippians 2:12) The phrase **work out** conveys the idea of working something through to its ultimate conclusion. The phrase was used in Paul's day of digging silver out of the mines. The silver was already in the mine, God put it there, they simply had to work it out. As believer's we are to **work out** what God has already worked in. Like a miner digs the precious metals out of the ground that God has put there for him, believers are to dig out of their salvation the precious nuggets of His grace. Just as there are no cheap shortcuts to mining, the Christian life will involve some work—that is some doing! Jesus said, **If ye know these things, happy are ye if ye do them. John 13:17**

A CROWN TO ATTAIN

For so an entrance shall be ministered unto you abundantly into the everlasting kingdom of our Lord and Saviour Jesus Christ. (2 Peter 1:11) The Christian who overcomes and lives victoriously here will be welcomed into Heaven in a wonderful way. It will be worth it to hear Jesus say, ... **Well done, thou good and faithful servant: thou hast been faithful over a few things, I will make thee ruler over many things: enter thou into the joy of thy lord. (Matthew 25:21)**

Why The Preacher Repeats Himself
2 Peter 1:12-15

It doesn't hurt anything to repeat the great truths of the Bible. Peter probably preached some of his sermons more than once. Vance Havner said that, *"There is no need to a sermon in moth balls once its preached."* One of the ways we learn is by repetition. The more we hear something, the better the chances are that we will retain it. Peter is seen here as a loving shepherd constantly reminding his flock of the great truths of the faith. The fact that Peter would soon pass from this life intensifies the seriousness of his warnings.

HIS ASSIGNED DUTY

Wherefore I will not be negligent to put you always in remembrance of these things, though ye know them, and be established in the present truth. (2 Peter 1:12) Peter had a keen awareness of his duty as a preacher. He did not want to be **negligent** with his duty to proclaim the truth. His desire was to be a faithful servant of the Lord and that involved reminding his flock of things that they had heard before and were even established in. The word **established** comes from *"sterizo"* and means *"to be fixed, set or strengthened."* The idea is that of setting someone up and strengthening him in the truth. Our Lord had charged Peter to ... **strengthen thy brethren. (Luke 22:32)** Many of the people to whom Peter wrote were mature believers, but they needed to be reminded of the great truths of Scripture. Even when believers are established in the truth it is easy to become cold in their zeal for the Lord. Such was the case with the Church of Ephesus. One of the saddest things on earth is when folks forsake the great doctrines of the faith that they were once established in, to go off after some foolishness that brings dishonor upon Christ. Paul had to deal with the Galatian believers about this very thing. Though once established in grace, they had gone back into legalism.

> **O foolish Galatians, who hath bewitched you, that ye should not obey the truth, before whose eyes Jesus Christ hath been evidently set forth, crucified among you? (Galatians 3:1)**

The word **bewitched** means *"to cast a spell over."* It carries the idea of being mesmerized or fascinated with something or someone. We are living in a day when even God's people are mesmerized and spell-bound with Personalities, Programs, and Performances rather than Principle. May God help is to get back to the Bible.

Peter made no apology for repeating himself. Peter was simply doing what God had called him to do. In fact, he would consider himself to be **negligent** if he didn't remind them of these things. The word **negligent** means *"to be careless or to make light of something."* Peter had been negligent in his duty when he failed to stand with Christ at His trial and crucifixion. He was determined to never again be guilty of such a thing. Brethren don't despise the preaching of God's word. Even if you are well established in the truth that is being preached, thank God for it. Just praise the Lord that truth is being preached.

HIS AFFIRMED DOCTRINE

Peter speaks of **present truth. (2 Peter 1:12)** The purpose of this book is to stir God's people concerning **these things** and warn of those who would deny, dispute, degrade and destroy truth. Peter knew the importance of building the believers up in doctrine. Doctrine is important to victory of the believer, as well as, to the life of the Church. The word doctrine simply means teaching and in the New Testament it refers to the body of teaching that Jesus and the Apostles handed down to Christians. Christ said, **Ye do err, not knowing the scriptures... (Matthew 22:29)** A Christian who has a firm grasp on truth will not be tossed to and fro, and carried about by every wind of doctrine. The Bible is the final authority in all matters of faith and practice. Christians must be built upon the eternal Word of God.

HIS APPROACHING DEATH

Knowing that shortly I must put off this my tabernacle, even as our Lord Jesus Christ hath shewed me. (2 Peter 1:14) Peter had a firm grip on the truth that preachers die but the word of God lives on. We are not here to build monuments to ourselves. This is about Christ. **He must increase, but I must decrease. (John 3:30)** Peter had no time to waste. He preached the truth and exalted Christ while there was opportunity. He said, **shortly I must put off this my tabernacle.** Peter uses the word **tabernacle** in reference to his body. That of a tent. A tent is a temporary dwelling place. When it is time to move on you just pull up the stakes, fold the tent and go. Peter knew that his death was imminent. Jesus told Peter years earlier about his coming death.

> **Verily, verily, I say unto thee, When thou wast young, thou girdedst thyself, and walkedst whither thou wouldest: but when thou shalt be old, thou shalt stretch forth thy hands, and another shall gird thee, and carry thee whither thou wouldest not. This spake he, signifying by what death he should glorify God. And when he had spoken this, he saith unto him, Follow me. (John 21:18-19)**

Knowing that a martyrs' death was coming did not deter Peter. In fact, it motivated him to speak out all the more. Peter knew that the day was coming when his tongue would be silenced. He would move on to glory, but he would also leave his opportunity to speak up for the Saviour and teach the word of God. In his first letter Peter reminded us that we are **strangers (1 Peter 1:1)** in this world. This word strangers speaks of one who is a *"pilgrim, sojourner, or foreigner."* It is a very descriptive term of what we are. We are foreigners to this world. This world is not our home we are mere strangers to here. The songwriter wrote:

> *This world is not my home, I'm just passing through.*
> *My treasures are laid up, Somewhere beyond the blue.*
> *The angels beckon me, From Heaven's open door,*
> *And I can't be at home, In this world anymore.*

Most believers are no longer living as a stranger to this world, they are living as settlers. We need to get back to a pilgrim status. By way of the new birth we are creatures of another world.

> **For here have we no continuing city, but we seek one to come. (Hebrews 13:14)**

Let us remember that this is about Jesus Christ:

> **Who gave himself for our sins, that he might deliver us from this present evil world, according to the will of God and our Father: (Galatians 1:4)**

The great Puritan Preacher, Richard Baxter said, *"I preach as never sure to preach again ... as a dying man to dying men."* Peter writes as a dying man to dying men. He knew that his voice would soon be silenced and his tongue would lie silent in the grave. He spoke up while he could.

HIS ABIDING DISCIPLES

Moreover I will endeavour that ye may be able after my decease to have these things always in remembrance. (2 Peter 1:15) The word **endeavour** comes from *"spoudazo"* and means *"to be diligent, to strive and to make every effort."* It carries the idea of striving earnestly to get something done. Peter was going to continue to diligently remind them of the great doctrines of the word. Even to the point that long after his death they would remember and stand on the truth of God's word.

Peter says, **that ye may be able after my decease to have these things always in remembrance. (2 Peter 1:15b)** The grave may silence our tongue but it doesn't have to end our influence. The day is coming when we will no longer be able to witness for Christ. We will no longer be here to instruct and direct our kids. We won't be around to encourage the hurting. All opportunity for earthly ministry will be over. Jesus said, **I must work the works of him that sent me, while it is day: the night cometh, when no man can work. (John 9:4)** The night is coming. May God help us to speak up for Him while we have opportunity. **Whatsoever thy hand findeth to do, do it with thy might; for there is no work, nor device, nor knowledge, nor wisdom, in the grave, whither thou goest. (Ecclesiastes 9:10)**

A More Sure Word
2 Peter 1:16-21

As Peter prepares to deal with prophetic events he first establishes the fact of the authority and accuracy of the word of God. The word of God is hated by many today. The labor in vain attempts to disprove the validity of the old book. But the child of God know the infinite value of God's word. It has been used of God to reveal to millions the way into the Kingdom. It has been at the scene of many revivals. It is the blessed Book that has comforted many hurting hearts. It is the lamp whereby we see to walk in this dark and sinful world. The Word of God is the final authority in all matters of faith and practice. **The grass withereth, the flower fadeth: but the word of our God shall stand for ever. (Isaiah 40:8)**

IT IS INFALLIBLE

For we have not followed cunningly devised fables, when we made known unto you the power and coming of our Lord Jesus Christ, but were eyewitnesses of his majesty. (2 Peter 1:16) We have God's word as opposed to **cunningly devised fables**. The word **fable** comes from *"mythos."* It is the word from which we get our word *"myth"* and speaks of a story of fiction. Peter assures his readers that what he had told them was not a cunningly devised fable based on some story or myth that he had heard, but rather the things that he had seen with his own eyes on the Mount of Transfiguration. Peter had seen Jesus Christ in His glory and at that same time also heard the audible voice of God the Father. **For he received from God the Father honour and glory, when there came such a voice to him from the excellent glory, This is my beloved Son, in whom I am well pleased. And this voice which came from heaven we heard, when we were with him in the holy mount. (2 Peter 1:17-18)** As believers we do not base our faith on clever stories and fairy tales. The false teacher did that and Peter deals with them in the next chapter. Instead, our faith rests upon the Inspired, Infallible, Inerrant word of God. Jesus said, **Man shall not live by bread alone, but by every word that proceedeth out of the mouth of God. (Matthew 4:4)** The first Baptist distinctive is Biblical Authority. As Baptists we insist that the Bible is the Word of God and the final authority in all matters of faith and practice. We do not rely upon hand me down tradition and manmade teachings. We simply take God at His Word—we believe and obey the Bible.

IT IS INCOMPARABLE

We have also a more sure word of prophecy ... (2 Peter 1:19a) The phrase **more sure** carries the idea of *firm, trustworthy and dependable.* The Bible is a proven book. The fables of the false teachers tickle ears and entertain, but the Word of God changes lives and endures forever. It is sad that so many are banking everything including their eternity on fables. **But the word of the Lord endureth for ever. And this is the word which by the gospel is preached unto you. (1 Peter 1:25)** The word of God is a permanent book and it will always be. Voltaire, the French infidel, said that within thirty years after his death the Bible would pass *"into the* *limbo of forgotten literature."* Today the very house in which Voltaire lived belongs to the French Bible Society and is used as a storehouse for Bibles. The very walls that once sheltered the skeptic infidel are now lined with copies of God's Word. How foolish to attempt the destruction of something that God has already determined will abide forever! **For ever, O LORD, thy word is settled in heaven. (Psalm 119:89)** It is certain that the devil hates God's Word. He has tried for centuries to destroy it along with the faith of millions. Many have pronounced its demise, but they're gone and faithful men are still proclaiming the Word of God every day. Jesus said, **Heaven and earth shall pass away: but my words shall not pass away. (Mark 13:31)** The enemies of God have come against the Bible with their blasphemous threatenings, but the Old Book has weathered every storm. Every opponent has been defeated. The Bible has been opened and read at the graves of its infidel enemies. **The grass withereth, the flower fadeth: but the word of our God shall stand for ever. (Isaiah 40:8)** The Bible confirms itself. God guarantees it and backs it with His name. The Psalmist said, **I will worship toward thy holy temple, and praise thy name for thy lovingkindness and for thy truth: for thou hast magnified thy word above all thy name. (Psalm 138:2)** It is an Incomparable book.

IT IS ILLUMINATING

Peter goes on to say ... **whereunto ye do well that ye take heed, as unto a light that shineth in a dark place, until the day dawn, and the day star arise in your hearts: (2 Peter 1:19)** Because the Bible is God's word we are to **take heed** to it. The word **heed** means *"to turn one's mind to pay* *attention to, be cautious about, apply oneself to, adhere to."* It is a word that has to do with our seriousness toward the word of God. The idea is that of being serious and giving our undivided attention to the word.

... as unto a light that shineth in a dark place, until the day dawn, and the day star arise in your hearts: (2 Peter 1:19) The metaphor here speaks volumes. Peter speaks of the word of God as **a light that shineth in a dark place.** The phrase **dark place** speaks of the evil and wickedness of this depravity stricken world—it is a dark place. We walk in a dark world and we need light. Peter reminds us that God's word is our light.

> **Thy word is a lamp unto my feet, and a light unto my path. (Psalm 119:105)**
>
> **The entrance of thy words giveth light; it giveth understanding unto the simple. (Psalm 119:130)**
>
> **For the commandment is a lamp; and the law is light; and reproofs of instruction are the way of life: (Proverbs 6:23)**

Peter says, **until the day dawn, and the day star arise in your hearts.** Until our Lord returns the word of God is our primary source of light in this dark world.

IT IS INDEPENDENT

Knowing this first, that no prophecy of the scripture is of any private interpretation. (2 Peter 1:20) The bible is a self-contained book. It is not up to us to see what we can make out of the Bible. We must study and rightly divide the word of truth. Many take a verse from here and a verse from there and come up with their own concoction of confusion and chaos. The Bible must be studied as a whole comparing passage with passage. The Psalmist said, **Through thy precepts I get understanding... (Psalm 119:104)** As we study the Word the Holy Spirit opens our understanding. **The entrance of thy words giveth light; it giveth understanding to the simple. (Psalm 119:130)** It is dangerous to just grab a verse and run with it. Many a false doctrine has been taught that way. We must search the Scriptures. Speaking of the Bereans, Paul said, **These were more noble than those in Thessalonica, in that they received the word with all readiness of mind, and searched the scriptures daily, whether those things were so. (Acts 17:11)**

IT IS INSPIRED

For the prophecy came not in old time by the will of man: but holy men of God spake as they were moved by the Holy Ghost. (2 Peter 1:21) The prophets and writers whose works are recorded in our Bible wrote under the guidance and control of God.. Their message was not of their own invention. What they communicated was the very Word of God. God so carried along the writers of Scripture that what they wrote were the very words God intended to use to convey His message to man. Thus the words of the Bible, not the writers, are said to be inspired. **All scripture is given by inspiration of God... (2 Timothy 3:16a)** The three words *"inspiration of God"* comes from one word, *"Theopneustos"*, and literally means *"God breathed."* All Scripture is God breathed. We have an inspired Bible. God has magnified His word above His name. **I will worship toward thy holy temple, and praise thy name for thy**

lovingkindness and for thy truth: for thou hast magnified thy word above all thy name. (Psalm 138:2) God has promised to keep His Word pure and preserved.

> The words of the LORD are pure words: as silver tried in a furnace of earth, purified seven times. Thou shalt keep them, O LORD, thou shalt preserve them from this generation for ever. (Psalms 12: 6-7)
>
> The grass withereth, the flower fadeth: but the word of our God shall stand for ever. (Isaiah 40:8)
>
> Being born again, not of corruptible seed, but of incorruptible, by the word of God, which liveth and abideth for ever. (1 Peter 1:23)

There have been many attacks on the old book, but it has withstood every assault.

False Teachers
2 Peter 2:1-3

As we turn to the second chapter we notice a strong change in the tone of Peter's writing. Peter sets out to warn God's people about the onslaught of false teachers and the rise of apostasy. Remember, though Peter is the human penman, it is the Holy Spirit Who is behind the writing and He saw fit to give us this warning. Apostasy is a much avoided subject in our day, but one that is greatly needed.

THEIR DISGUISE

But there were false prophets also among the people, even as there shall be false teachers among you ... (2 Peter 2:1a) These false teachers are seen as being **among the people** and **among you.** These are wolves in sheep's clothing that disguise themselves as part of the flock. These men are clearly identified as **false prophets**. The term **prophet** is a religious term. The word **false** identifies them as counterfeit. They were religious, but they weren't real. You will notice that Peter doesn't mince words in dealing with these apostates. He uses Serious, Scathing and Straightforward language to describe these false teachers. Jesus also used strong words when He warned about false prophets. **Beware of false prophets, which come to you in sheep's clothing, but inwardly they are ravening wolves. Matthew 7:15** The Apostle Paul warned, **For I know this, that after my departing shall grievous wolves enter in among you, not sparing the flock. Also of your own selves shall men arise, speaking perverse things, to draw away disciples after them. (Acts 20:29-30)** These false prophets infiltrate the church and pretend to be of the Lord, but they are Deceitful, Dangerous and Destructive. Jude described them as **... certain men crept in unawares, who were before of old ordained to this condemnation, ungodly men, turning the grace of our God into lasciviousness, and denying the only Lord God, and our Lord Jesus Christ (Jude 1:4)** The phrase **crept in unawares** carries the idea of *"settling in alongside of ... to enter secretly, slip in quietly."* These apostates secretly slip in and settle down in the Church with their wicked intentions to destroy, divide and divert the loyalty of God's people to themselves. Raleigh Campbell says:

> "It speaks of seeping gradually into the minds of these people. It indicates a secret, stealthy and subtle intrusion into the state of church life and the personal faith with the intent of undermining and breaking down their beliefs and convictions."

This is how these wicked men work. They come to Church, sit in the worship services and Sunday-school classes, attend the Church fellowships, etc. They are part of the everyday life of the Church except for one important thing—they are imposters. They are not present for the good of the Church, but for the destruction of it. The desire of the apostate is to destroy the old-time region and gain a following for himself.

THEIR DECEPTION

Peter warns that these false teachers **... privily shall bring in damnable heresies (2 Peter 2:1b)** False teachers are an underhanded bunch. The word **privily** speaks to do something in a secret and sneaky fashion. The Greek is *pareisagō* and means "to bring in by the side of." It carries the idea of twisting, turning and maneuvering in order to get something through the door. This is how they work. They twist and turn and warp the truth gradually indoctrinating people. Notice that they are **damnable heresies**. What they peddle tickles ears, but it damns the soul and destroys the saint. They set out to destroy the truth while at the same time leading multitudes into the pit of Hell.

THEIR DENIAL

… even denying the Lord that bought them, and bring upon themselves swift destruction. (2 Peter 2:1c) False teachers have no problem attacking the Saviour Who shed His blood for them. They refuse His payment for sin. The word **bought** means to redeem. The word **denying** is a strong term of contempt. It means *"to refuse and to have nothing to do with."* Though false teachers may use our terminology the fact of the matter is they want nothing to do with Christ. The so-called Jehovah's Witnesses speak of the Son of God, but their definition is far different from what the Bible teaches. We are seeing this on all fronts today. Liberal theology regularly denies the Deity of Christ, His blood atonement, His bodily resurrection, His virgin birth, His sinlessness, His literal return and His miracles. False teachers are working behind the scenes trying to do away with the truths that are fundamental to our Christianity.

THEIR DISCIPLES

And many shall follow their pernicious ways … (2 Peter 2:2a) Notice that **MANY**, not a few, but **many follow** them. The word **follow** means *"to conform to and imitate."* These followers make gods of their false teachers. It is not so surprising that these false teachers have so many followers. They are peddling an easy chair religion that many are looking for. Jude gives us some insight into the reason for their popularity. **For there are certain men crept in unawares, who were before of old ordained to this condemnation, ungodly men, turning the grace of our God into lasciviousness, and denying the only Lord God, and our Lord Jesus Christ. (Jude 1:4)** Take note of that little phrase **turning the grace of our God into lasciviousness.** The word, **lasciviousness** means *"looseness; irregular indulgence of animal desires; wantonness; lustfulness"* According to Vines, The prominent idea is *"shameless conduct."* It carries the idea of living without restraint. It is living according to lustful desires. But notice that they don't just live a **lasciviousness** lifestyle, they are **turning the grace of our God into lasciviousness.** They turn the grace of God into a license to sin. They use the excuse of *"being under grace"* to justify their wicked lifestyles. They even poke fun at and mark as weird those who hold to the old-time religion. These grace perverters call old fashioned Christians *"legalists"* while they indulge in the pleasure of this wicked world. They teach that grace allows their lifestyle. We have in our day a brand of salvation being preached that is dangerous. Theirs is a way of no repentance, no righteousness and no rules. It is a perverted grace and the Bible condemns it. Still many follow them into destruction.

THEIR DISGRACE

... their pernicious ways; by reason of whom the way of truth shall be evil spoken of. (2 Peter 2:2b) Their **pernicious** ways speak of their destructive behavior. Belief

False Teachers

always effects behavior. When one doesn't think right about Christ he won't live right. **For as he thinketh in his heart, so is he ... (Proverbs 23:7)** As a result of a religious profession, but a wicked lifestyle, **the way of truth shall be evil spoken of.** False teachers bring reproach upon the name of Christ. They cause people to speak evil of God, Christ, the Church and Christians. One of the reactions folks have when you invite them to Church is the old excuse, "That church is full of hypocrites." Well it probably is not full of hypocrites, maybe a few. All Churches seem to have a few. Anyway, where do you think folks get that idea? Not from everyone in the Church, but from one or two who's lifestyle don't match their profession. As a result everything that is precious to God is blasphemed and evil spoken of.

THEIR DEALINGS

And through covetousness shall they with feigned words make merchandise of you ... (2 Peter 2:3a) The word covetousness speaks of the desire to have more. These false teachers are in it for what they can get out of it. They want material gain and wealth and you usually don't get that preaching the whole counsel of God. So they use **feigned words make merchandise of you.** The word **feigned** means *artificial.* They use these artificial words for the purpose of making **merchandise of you.** They tell folks what they want to hear for the purpose of **getting ahead.** Solomon said, **A man that flattereth his neighbour spreadeth a net for his feet (Proverbs 29:5)** The word flattery means to *"speak smoothly."* Flattery is insincere smooth talk that that these false teachers and apostates us as a means of controlling others.

THEIR DAMNATION

...whose judgment now of a long time lingereth not, and their damnation slumbereth not. (2 Peter 2:3b) We are assured that God has the last word on the matter. Throughout history God has condemned and promised judgment on those who distort His truth. The phrase **lingereth not** is a solemn phrase. The word **lingereth** carries the idea of being idle. The phrase means that God's judgment is not idle. The idea is that God's judgment of these apostate false teachers is actively accumulating wrath until the great white throne judgment. The words Peter uses for **judgment** and **damnation** are drawn from the courtroom. They are judicial terms. In this verse God is seen as the Judge who hands down the sentence of Hell. **Damnation** is seen an executioner, awake, alert and ready to carry out God's sentence.

God's Judgment On False Teachers
2 Peter 2:4-9

The last section closes with the solemn words, **...whose judgment now of a long time lingereth not, and their damnation slumbereth not. (2 Peter 2:3b)** It is for certain that God will judge false teachers. He hold them accountable for every soul that they had led astray.

THE DEMONSTRATION OF JUDGMENT

Having pronounced God's judgment on these false teachers, Peter goes back to the book of Genesis and pulls out three examples of God's judgment as examples. These examples serve as a solemn warning to the false teachers as well as offer proof to those who didn't take him seriously (2 Peter 3:3-4)

The Unholy Angels

For if God spared not the angels that sinned, but cast them down to hell, and delivered them into chains of darkness, to be reserved unto judgment; (2 Peter 2:4) Peter's first example is the judgment of the Angels who rebelled with Satan. Jude used the same example when he wrote concerning God's judgment on apostasy. **And the angels which kept not their first estate, but left their own habitation, he hath reserved in everlasting chains under darkness unto the judgment of the great day. (Jude 1:6)** This example takes us back to Satan's rebellion and fall

(Isaiah 14:12-17; Ezekiel 28:12-19) At the time of Satan's fall he persuaded one third (Revelation 12:4) of the angels of heaven to rebel with him. It was at this time that Hell was created and it was these angels that Christ spoke of. **Then shall he say also unto them on the left hand, Depart from me, ye cursed, into everlasting fire, prepared for the devil and his angels (Matthew 25:41)** These angels exchanged their place in Heaven with God for a place in Hell with Satan. What a startling example of how destructive apostasy is.

The Unrepentant World

And spared not the old world, but saved Noah the eighth person, a preacher of righteousness, bringing in the flood upon the world of the ungodly; (2 Peter 2:5) The **old world** refers to God's original creation.

> **And GOD saw that the wickedness of man was great in the earth, and that every imagination of the thoughts of his heart was only evil continually. And it repented the LORD that he had made man on the earth, and it grieved him at his heart. And the LORD said, I will destroy man whom I have created from the face of the earth; both man, and beast, and the creeping thing, and the fowls of the air; for it repenteth me that I have made them ... And God said unto Noah, The end of all flesh is come before me; for the earth is filled with violence through them; and, behold, I will destroy them with the earth. (Genesis 6:5-7, 13)**

The antediluvian (pre-flood) civilization was wholly given over to wickedness. Sinful man had become so wicked **that**

every imagination of the thoughts of his heart was only evil continually. (Genesis 6:5)

Even after God's decision to destroy the earth, He gave wicked man one hundred and twenty years longer to repent. But stubborn and prideful man repented not. He chose his sin over the salvation. Because of man's wickedness, God destroyed every person and every land animal (except for Noah and his family) in His judgment. He covered the entire earth with water—even the tops of the highest mountains. **And the waters prevailed exceedingly upon the earth; and all the high hills, that were under the whole heaven, were covered. Fifteen cubits upward did the waters prevail; and the mountains were covered. (Genesis 7:19-20)** We are seeing a repeat of this kind of wickedness in our day. Jesus said we would.

> **But as the days of Noe *were*, so shall also the coming of the Son of man be. For as in the days that were before the flood they were eating and drinking, marrying and giving in marriage, until the day that Noe entered into the ark, And knew not until the flood came, and took them all away; so shall also the coming of the Son of man be. (Matthew 24:37-39)**

This is the time that Jesus referred to as the days of Noah. The wickedness of those days parallels the evil of our day. Notice in our text that Peter referred to the society of that day as **the world of the ungodly; (2 Peter 2:5)** The word for **ungodly** is "*asebes*" and speaks of irreverence, sinfulness. It carries the idea of a complete lack of reverence, worship or fear of God. We are seeing it all over in our day. The antediluvians would have been saved if they would have repented. They heard Noah preach and they watched him for 120 years as he built the ark. Yet, they repented not.

The Unrighteous Cities

And turning the cities of Sodom and Gomorrha into ashes condemned them with an overthrow, making them an ensample unto those that after should live ungodly; (2 Peter 2:6) The third example comes from the damnation of Sodom and Gomorrah and carries with it a stern warning for us today. Again, Jude uses the same example. **"Even as Sodom and Gomorrha, and the cities about them in like manner, giving themselves over to fornication, and going after strange flesh, are set forth for an example, suffering the vengeance of eternal fire" (Jude 1:7)** Genesis 19:4-14 describes the awful filth that characterized the men of Sodom and Gomorrah. They were politically correct, but they were wicked and lost. In Geneses 19 we have the account of two Angels visiting Lot at his house in Sodom. The people of the city came to the house and demanded that Lot turn over his visitors for their wicked intentions. Can you imagine this? Wicked men so caught up in their sin that they would rape Angels sent by God. The Bible says, **Then the LORD rained upon Sodom and upon Gomorrah brimstone and fire from the LORD out of heaven; And he overthrew those cities, and all the plain, and all the inhabitants of the cities, and that which grew upon the ground. (Genesis 19:24-25)** No one ever gets away with sin.

What a warning for our day. God will not spare apostate false teachers. He did not spare the apostates before the flood and He will not spare apostates after the flood. God did not withhold His judgment.

THE DELIVERANCE FROM JUDGMENT

(For that righteous man dwelling among them, in seeing and hearing, vexed his righteous soul from day to day with their unlawful deeds;) The Lord knoweth how to deliver the godly out of temptations, and to reserve the unjust unto the day of judgment to be punished: (2 Peter 2:8-9) Peter says that Lot **vexed his righteous soul from day to day with their unlawful deeds (2 Peter 2:8)** The word vexed means *"tormented and distressed."* It carries the idea of being weighed down and wore out. Lot was tormented and distressed by the overwhelming depravity all around him. He should have never went to Sodom, but certainly he should have left as soon as he saw the wickedness. He did not leave. Like many of God's people of today, Lot kept his mouth shut and blended in with the world. Lot paid a big price for his disobedience. It cost him his walk with God. He lost his family to the world. He lost his wife. Even his daughters who came out with him brought the philosophies and practices of Sodom with them. If Abraham hadn't interceded for him, Lot would have died with the sodomites.

Notice also that Lot had a **righteous soul.** Lot was a saved man. He never got involved in the wicked practices of the Sodomites but he did tolerate it though he was repulsed by it. It weighed him down and wore him out, but he stayed there. Remember that it was largely a financial decision that landed him there. But Lot, nevertheless, was a **righteous** man. He wasn't righteous because of his actions, but because of his faith. He had a righteous standing before God. I am thankful that as believers our sins are gone and we have the imputed righteousness of Christ. What a security!

The Lord knoweth how to deliver the godly out of temptations. (2 Peter 2:8-9) I am very thankful that the Deliverance of the righteous is as certain as the Destruction of the wicked. The child of God has no part in the judgment of the wicked.

The Consequences Of Heresy
2 Peter 2:10-16

Peter didn't play around when he warned us against false teachers and perils of heresy. He used some of the most scathing language of the Bible to denounce the heretics and their heresy. He spoke very pointedly about the effect that false teaching heretics would have on people. He warned of the disillusionment and defeat that would follow for those who were taken in by such heresy. One's life will always follow his belief. **For as he thinketh in his heart, so is he ... (Proverbs 23:7)** If a person believes wrong, he or she will live wrong. Here Peter deals with the consequences of listening to false teachers. If you listen to them you will eventually embrace their teaching. When you embrace their teaching your life will follow. Notice the Consequences Of Heresy as it is seen in the lifestyle of these false teachers.

THEY ARE INSUBORDINATE

But chiefly them that walk after the flesh in the lust of uncleanness, and despise government. selfwilled, they are not afraid to speak evil of dignities. (2 Peter 2:10) In this one verse Peter gives us four characteristics of these false teachers and those who embrace their heresy.

Their Drive

The first thing about these guys is that they **walk after the flesh in the lust of uncleanness.** They are driven by depravity. They are not walking in the Spirit. Paul said,

...Walk in the Spirit, and ye shall not fulfil the lust of the flesh. (Galatians 5:16) Remember that these are false teachers. They deny the Deity of Christ, the Inspiration and authority of Scripture and many other precious doctrines of the Bible. These false teachers are lost. They do not have the Spirit. They are doing what comes natural to them—they are walking in the flesh.

Their Demeanor

Peter says that these false teachers and their followers are **Presumptuous ...** The word **presumptuous** comes from *"tolmetes "*and is used only here. It speaks of being *"shamelessly and boldly arrogant."* So brazen are these false teachers that they defy God and exalt themselves. It is common today to see preachers and teachers who set themselves up as god in the life of their followers. Like Diotrephes they want preeminence for themselves.

> **I wrote unto the church: but Diotrephes, who loveth to have the preeminence among them, receiveth us not. 3 John 1:9**

Diotrephes was driven by the flesh and motivated by pride. Jesus Christ alone is to have such preeminence. God has determined **...that in all things he might have the preeminence. Colossians 1:18** A person who walks in the Spirit will say with John the Baptist, **"He must increase, but I must decrease" (John 3:30)**

Their Determination

These guys are **selfwilled...** the word selfwilled comes from *"authades"* and carries the idea self-pleasing. These people live for themselves. They do what pleases them and they are obstinate about it. They refuse to listen to reason. They are set on doing what they want, and nothing is going to stop them. They are self-willed and stubborn refusing to submit to the authority of God's word.

Their Disdain

We see in our text that they also **despise government** and **they are not afraid to speak evil of dignities.** Jude made the same charge. **Likewise also these filthy dreamers defile the flesh, despise dominion, and speak evil of dignities. (Jude 1:8)** The words **government** and **dominion** speak of authority. These words speak of those in authority and speaks of someone of honorable rank or position. The word **despise** means *"to scorn; to disdain; to have the lowest opinion of."* The phrase **speak evil** comes from *"blasphemeo"* from which we get our English word *"blasphemy."* It carries the idea of slander. False teachers and those who follow them have no respect for God ordained authority.

As a result of pridefully and stubbornly living for themselves they arrogantly refuse to recognize God-ordained authority. God has clearly established a system of authority. God Himself is the ultimate authority (Deuteronomy 11:27; Jeremiah 11:4, 7; Zechariah 6:15) God has given authority to husbands (Ephesians 5:22-23, 1 Peter 3:1), to parents (Ephesians 6:1, Colossians 3:20) and to government (Romans 13:1-7). He has also given authority to pastors (Hebrews 13:7, 17). Our God is a God of order and to have order there must be authority. You can tell a whole lot about a person by how he respects and responds to authority.

Their Daring

Whereas angels, which are greater in power and might, bring not railing accusation against them before the Lord. (2 Peter 2:11) What a contrast. Jude, speaking in the same context, gives us an example. **Yet Michael the archangel, when contending with the devil he disputed about the body of Moses, durst not bring against him a railing accusation, but said, The Lord rebuke thee. (Jude 1:10)** These false teachers do that which even the highest angel would not dare do. Even Michael himself would not rebuke the devil. This is the only place in the Bible where this particular incident is mentioned. Therefore, we cannot know the full details of Michael's dispute with Satan. However, we do know that when Moses died God took full charge of the funeral and carried it out in secret. **So Moses the servant of the LORD died there in the land of Moab, according to the word of the LORD. And he buried him in a valley in the land of Moab, over against Bethpeor: but no man knoweth of his sepulchre unto this day. (Deuteronomy 34:5-6)** God probably sent Michael the archangel with instructions concerning the burial of Moses. Michael ranks first in God's creative order of angels. His name means *"who is as God."* As he was carrying out God's orders the devil showed up and began to argue with him over the body. Some suggest that Satan wanted the body of Moses to lure Israel into further idolatry. This is probably true since man is so inclined to worship relics and leftovers. This incident is used as a contrast, Michael was acting under the direct authority of God. The devil was acting under his own usurped authority. Michael was diligent about carrying out the orders of God. Notice that Satan was just as diligent to hinder him. However, Michael contends faithfully against the devil, never wavering and never using his own authority. He **durst not bring against him a railing accusation, but said, The Lord rebuke thee.** Our authority to contend for the faith is a delegated authority and we must rely upon the God Who delegated it to us.

THEY ARE IRRATIONAL

But these, as natural brute beasts, made to be taken and destroyed, speak evil of the things that they understand not; and shall utterly perish in their own corruption. (2 Peter 2:12) These false teachers are compared to **"natural brute beasts."** Peter illustrates the nature of false teachers by comparing them to animals that have no reason. They are driven by instinct rather than understanding. Animals don't think it over, they just do what comes naturally. Like animals these false teachers are slaves to their instinct. Their nature is to peddle false doctrine.

Peter says, **made to be taken and destroyed. (2 Peter 2:12b)** On the day of slaughter an animal will go on eating, sleeping and doing the things it does naturally. It is not rational it is instinct—it is his nature. Apostates have no concern for the judgment to come. They are living for the flesh. James said, **"Ye have lived in pleasure on the earth, and been wanton; ye have nourished your hearts, as in a day of slaughter" (James 5:5)**

These false teachers **speak evil of the things that they understand not. (2 Peter 2:12c)** The phrase **speak evil** comes from *"blasphemeo"* from which we get our English word *"blasphemy."* It carries the idea of slander. Slander is an attempt to discredit or defame. False teachers attempt to discredit the precious truths of the word of God. These are truths that **"they understand not."** Some of these false teachers have great minds and degrees, but they are powerless to understand the word of God. **"But the natural man receiveth not the things of the Spirit of God: for they are foolishness unto him: neither can he know them, because they are spiritually discerned" (1 Corinthians 2:14)** They may have a PhD, but they need the Holy Spirit to know and understand the Bible. **Because the carnal mind is enmity against God: for it is not subject to the law of God, neither indeed can be. So then they that are in the flesh cannot please God. (Romans 8:7-8)** No matter how much education a man has the Bible is a closed book to him apart from the enabling of the Spirit of God.

Peter says, **and shall utterly perish in their own corruption. And shall receive the reward of unrighteousness, as they that count it pleasure to riot in the day time. Spots they are and blemishes, sporting themselves with their own deceivings while they feast with you. (2 Peter 2:12d-13)** False teachers will not escape God's wrath. They go on as natural brute beasts, destroying and defaming the truth of God's word, but the judgment of God is coming. Like an animal in the day of slaughter, apostates will be dealt with finally and fully.

THEY ARE IMMORAL

Having eyes full of adultery, and that cannot cease from sin; beguiling unstable souls: an heart they have exercised with covetous practices; cursed children. (2 Peter 2:14) Never have we seen a time when so many religious teachers are falling into sexual sin. **Having eyes full of adultery**

indicates that these false teachers can't even look at a woman without seeing her as an object of fornication. This reminds us of the words of Christ. **But I say unto you, That whosoever looketh on a woman to lust after her hath committed adultery with her already in his heart. (Matthew 5:28)** The heart is where adultery starts and the eyes are the gateway to the heart. Jeremiah said, **Mine eye affecteth mine heart because of all the daughters of my city. (Lamentations 3:51)**

They are so entangled that they **cannot cease from sin.** They are slaves to their desires. They are so driven by their wicked desires that they can't stop. They are powerless to overcome.

They go on, **beguiling unstable souls.** The word **beguiling** means to *"entice or to entrap."* It is a sportsman's term that speaks of using a lure to entice a fish to bite at the hidden hook. These deceptive false teachers entice and lure others into their wickedness. They are predators of the worst sort because they hide themselves under the cloak of religion. The word unstable comes from *"astēriktos"* and speaks of those who are *"immature and indecisive in their faith, easily led astray"* (Renn's Expository Dictionary of Bible Words)

THEY ARE INSINCERE

"Which have forsaken the right way, and are gone astray, following the way of Balaam the son of Bosor, who loved the wages of unrighteousness; But was rebuked for his iniquity: the dumb ass speaking with man's voice forbad the madness of the prophet" (2 Peter 2:15-16) They are in it for what they can get out of it. Their interest is not helping people—they are after personal gain. Peter illustrates by using Balaam as an example. The story of

Balaam is found in Numbers 22-24 and 31. Baalam was a prophet who sold out for money. He was hired by the king of Moab to pronounce curses upon Israel. God intervened and stopped him from succeeding and reversed the whole thing and caused Balaam to pronounce the blessing of the Lord upon the people of Israel instead. When he realized that he had failed to accomplish his original purpose, Balaam recommended to the Midianites that they lure the Israelites into Baal worship. The men of Israel fell for it and 24,000 of them died under God's judgment. He was driven by a desire for personal gain.

Pulpits are full of Balaams today! Apostates are out for all they can get. They are not interested in helping God's people. They simply want their paychecks and will not do anything that might offend the sinners in their congregation. They are not real shepherds, if they were they would preach the Word of God regardless of the consequences. John describes the hireling, **"But he that is an hireling, and not the shepherd, whose own the sheep are not, seeth the wolf coming, and leaveth the sheep, and fleeth: and the wolf catcheth them, and scattereth the sheep. The hireling fleeth, because he is an hireling, and careth not for the sheep" (John 10:12-13)** These are not true shepherds, their true love is money, they stay until things get a little rough and then go on their way.

Empty Wells, Vomiting Dogs And Wallowing Hogs

2 Peter 2:17-22

Peter uses three analogies to drive his point home concerning false teachers. The imagery here aptly describes the spiritual depravity and dearth of those who reject God and follow their own course.

THEIR CLAIM EXAMINED

These are wells without water, clouds that are carried with a tempest; to whom the mist of darkness is reserved for ever. (2 Peter 2:17) False teachers often have the ability speak great swelling words. They are often highly educated and eloquently capture the hearts of their hearers but their claims are empty and worthless. Peter uses two illustrations to describe the worthlessness of their claims.

Peter says that these false teachers are like **wells without water. (2 Peter 2:17a)** Water is a precious commodity that we often take for granted. This was not so in Bible days. Water was a priceless treasure. Water was a symbol of life and salvation in Israel. Where there was no water there was no life! The thought here is of a pilgrim travelling in the dessert. Hot and thirsty he drudges along. At last, out there in the distance he sees a well. He gathers all the strength he has left and pushes ahead until he reaches the well. But he finds it to be dry. There is nothing to quench his thirst.

False teachers are further described as **clouds that are carried with a tempest. (2 Peter 2:17b)** Again this describes the worthlessness of the apostate. Jude used the same illustration when he said, **... clouds they are without water, carried about of winds. (Jude 1:12)** This is a fitting picture of the false teacher! The idea here is of a drought stricken land, The drought has taken its toll on the crop. The sun is blistering hot, and the ground is dry and cracked. Everything is scorched and dying. The time is critical. Without rain the crops will soon be dead and all lost. Then yonder in the distance, clouds begin to form and roll in over the fields. What a sight! Rain, at last! But not so. Hours later the clouds have cleared and there is still no rain. Only a false hope.

What an apt description of false teachers. A false hope is all the false teacher has to offer. They are empty of anything that has spiritual value. They bring nothing but dearth and death. Empty wells and wind clouds. From a distance they appear to be genuine but after all is said and done, there is nothing but emptiness, the water of life has been withheld.

> **For my people have committed two evils; they have forsaken me the fountain of living waters, and hewed them out cisterns, broken cisterns, that can hold no water. (Jeremiah 2:13)**

For when they speak great swelling words of vanity, they allure through the lusts of the flesh, through much

wantonness, those that were clean escaped from them who live in error. (2 Peter 2:18)** The phrase **great swelling** describes the extravagant and flamboyant rhetoric that false teachers use to draw followers into their deception. They have nothing of true spiritual quality to offer. They manipulate and infatuate with their words and oratory skills. But regardless of their words, the Holy Spirit uses the word **vanity** to describe their message. Their message is vain, empty and worthless. Theirs is a message of death rather than life.

Peter says, **they allure through the lusts of the flesh, through much wantonness. (2 Peter 2:18b)** The word **allure** carries the idea of *"enticing and entrapping."* The words **lusts** and **wantonness** speak of *"desire, craving, lust, or longing."* False teachers use man's inborn depravity to bait their followers. They know how to appeal to the flesh in order to capture the heart. We are seeing a lot of this kind of apostasy. False teachers are offering the world a religion of no repentance, no righteousness and no rules. Unfortunately, it is also a religion without redemption and regeneration.

Look who they are largely preying on, **those that were clean escaped from them who live in error. (2 Peter 2:18c)** Their victims are not mature Christians and may not be Christians at all. It is speaking of those who have had some experience with the church, but have fallen away and who now **live in error.** They know just enough about the Bible to be religious and they have left the Church and are out on their own. False teachers prey on these.

There is an important lesson here. Satan loves to separate folks from the Church and get them out there alone where he can close in and attack. Even with the temptation of Christ in Matthew 4, Satan waited until Christ was alone in the wilderness before he attacked. Jesus didn't have anyone to encourage Him or to counsel Him. Every time Satan had ever seen Jesus he was in the presence of the Father and the Angels. But this time the Devil saw Jesus out there alone and considered it a good opportunity to attack. The Devil is cunning and crafty. He loves to get people alone and then attack. Eve was alone when she was tempted in the garden. David was alone when he was tempted on the rooftop. The Bible says that the Devil **... as a roaring lion, walketh about, seeking whom he may devour. (1 Peter 5:8)** The picture is of a lion on the prowl looking for just the right opportunity to pounce on his prey. One of the first things a lion will do when he comes upon a herd of antelope is to separate one of them from the rest of the herd. Once he separates the one from the safety of the herd he has no trouble picking him off. That is how Satan works. Isn't it amazing that as soon as Christians get a little discouraged the first thing they do is stop going to Church. Where do you think that idea comes from? It comes from Satan. The lion is trying to separate you from the source of your encouragement and strength. If you let Satan separate you from Church and fellowship you will soon be lunch for the lion.

THEIR CORRUPTION EXHIBITED

While they promise them liberty, they themselves are the servants of corruption: for of whom a man is overcome, of the same is he brought in bondage. (2 Peter

2:19) One of the favorite topics of these false teachers is liberty. These false teachers cry out, *"Now that you are under grace you don't have to have stands and convictions. Every goes! Enjoy your liberty."* These false teachers promise and promote liberty, but theirs is not true liberty for they themselves are **servants of corruption**. Today's Laodicean Liberty is used to cover a lot of sin and worldliness. However, we must reject such an idea and realize that our Christian liberty is not a license to sin.

> **For, brethren, ye have been called unto liberty; only use not liberty for an occasion to the flesh, but by love serve one another. (Galatians 5:13)**

Paul clears things up a bit in this verse. Paul said, **use not liberty for an occasion to the flesh.** This is in essence what the libertines of today are doing. They are using their brand of liberty to feed and satisfy worldly and ungodly desires. They teach that the grace of God allows their lifestyle. The Scripture warns us of such men.

> **For there are certain men crept in unawares, who were before of old ordained to this condemnation, ungodly men, turning the grace of our God into lasciviousness, and denying the only Lord God, and our Lord Jesus Christ. (Jude 1:4)**

Notice that they turned the grace of our God into lasciviousness. The word **lasciviousness** means *"unrestrained."* It carries the idea of having a *"license to live as one desires."* Theirs is a corrupting of the grace of God by turning it into nothing more than a license to sin by living an unrestrained lifestyle. Jude stated that in living such a lifestyle they were, **denying the only Lord God, and our Lord Jesus Christ.** You cannot live for the pleasures and sins of this world and claim Christ as your Saviour. Such a lifestyle is a denial of the Lord.

The principle of Christian liberty is clearly taught in the word of God. However, liberty is never the freedom to live any way you want to. Nor is it the freedom to ignore the clear commands of God's word. Jesus said, **If ye continue in my word, then are ye my disciples indeed; And ye shall know the truth, and the truth shall make you free. (John 8:31-32)** Liberty is always based upon the Word of God. **And I will walk at liberty: for I seek thy precepts. (Psalm 119:45)** Christian liberty does not ignore the moral law of God. Law and liberty go hand in hand. You cannot separate one from the other.

For if after they have escaped the pollutions of the world through the knowledge of the Lord and Saviour Jesus Christ, they are again entangled therein, and overcome, the latter end is worse with them than the beginning. (2 Peter 2:20) The **they** of this verse is the same as the **they** of verse 19. Peter is continuing to describe the false teachers. These false teachers are described as having some knowledge of Jesus Christ and even escaped the pollution of the world. However, they were not saved. After their profession they had been **entangled** and **overcome** in the same pollutions they had once escaped. The view that these are unsaved false teachers fits the context. They are the same ones described as those **... to whom the mist of darkness is reserved for ever. (2 Peter 2:17)** Remember, Judas had a knowledge of the Lord and even left the pollutions of the world and lived as a disciple, but he was lost. So are these false teachers.

For it had been better for them not to have known the way of righteousness, than, after they have known it, to turn from the holy commandment delivered unto them. (2 Peter 2:21) Reformation without regeneration only leads to a greater judgment. The knowledge that a person gathers as he is learning makes him more accountable when he stands before Christ. They would have been better off not to even have known the truth, than to have had a knowledge of Christ and rejected it. Jesus dealt with this same issue.

> **And whosoever shall not receive you, nor hear your words, when ye depart out of that house or city, shake off the dust of your feet. Verily I say unto you, It shall be more tolerable for the land of Sodom and Gomorrha in the day of judgment, than for that city. (Matthew 10:14-15)**

> When the unclean spirit is gone out of a man, he walketh through dry places, seeking rest, and findeth none. Then he saith, I will return into my house from whence I came out; and when he is come, he findeth it empty, swept, and garnished. Then goeth he, and taketh with himself seven other spirits more wicked than himself, and they enter in and dwell there: and the last state of that man is worse than the first. Even so shall it be also unto this wicked generation. (Matthew 12:43-45)

These false teachers had gained some knowledge of Christ and even swept their life clean of the world's pollutions, but the emptiness not replaced by the Holy Spirit. As a result their latter state was worse than their beginning.

THEIR CHARACTER EXEMPLIFIED

But it is happened unto them according to the true proverb, The dog is turned to his own vomit again; and the sow that was washed to her wallowing in the mire. (2 Peter 2:22) The dog returns to his vomit and the sow returns to her wallow because that is their nature. Clean them up, dress them up, teach them new tricks, but it is just outward. Nothing changes in their nature. The dog and the hog are just two other illustrations describing the emptiness and depravity of these false teachers.

End Time Scoffers
2 Peter 3:1-7

In chapter two, Peter spelled out the character of false teachers and the futility of their teaching. Now in chapter three Peter deals with the second coming of Jesus Christ and the end of the world. He starts off by warning us of the end-time scoffers.

THE SAINTS REALITY

Regardless of whether we like it or not, the reality is that there's a lot of false teaching out there today. These false teachers refuse to heed the word of God, repent and trust Christ. Peter describe these false teachers and their followers as **last days scoffers ... (2 Peter 3:3)** who **willingly are ignorant ... (2 Peter 3:5)** They have made a choice to be ignorant of the things of God go about scoffing the truth instead. Peter begins this chapter with instruction for the believer.

There Must Be Revival

Peter writes, **I now write unto you; in both which I stir up your pure minds ... (2 Peter 3:1a)** The words **stir up** comes from *diegeiro* carries the idea of *"awaken," "rouse from sleep."* The analogy of sleep is often used in the sense of spiritual apathy. The term awake is often used of revival. The believer of days gone called revival a Spiritual awakening. Paul uses this terminology often. Writing to the Romans Paul said, **And that, knowing the time, that now it is high time to awake out of sleep: for now is our salvation nearer than when we believed. Romans 13:11** To the

Thessalonians, **Therefore let us not sleep, as do others; but let us watch and be sober. (1 Thessalonians 5:6)** And to the Ephesians as well. **Wherefore he saith, Awake thou that sleepest, and arise from the dead, and Christ shall give thee light. (Ephesians 5:14)** The call to awake is the need of the hour. We have never experienced such an indifference toward spiritual matters as we see today. Leonard Ravenhill said that the tragedy of day is that *"Hell is burning while the Church sleeps."*

While God's people sleep the enemy works. The parable of the Sower says, **But while men slept, his enemy came and sowed tares among the wheat, and went his way. (Matthew 13:25)** That pretty much describes what is going on in our day. The devil is gaining a lot of ground while God's people slumber.

There Must Be Righteousness

Peter further speaks of stirring up our **pure minds (2 Peter 3:1b)** Only God's people can have pure minds. **Unto the pure all things are pure: but unto them that are defiled and unbelieving is nothing pure; but even their mind and conscience is defiled. (Titus 1:15)** Salvation cleans us up, but there must be a continual cleansing of the heart and mind through the study of God's Word. Jesus said, **Now ye are clean through the word which I have spoken unto you. (John 15:3)** God intends that we believers be a people of purity.

The word **pure** comes from the compound word *"eilikrines."* The word *"eile"* means *"sunlight"* and *"krino"* means *"to judge."* The idea is to be judged or tested by the sunlight. It is a word that comes from the pottery profession of Bible times. Pottery often developed cracks while being fired. Crooked merchants would fill the cracks with wax and paint over it. An soon as something hot was put in the pottery the wax would melt. In order to determine if a piece of pottery had been filled with wax the buyer would hold it up to the sunlight to examine it. If the piece had been cracked and filled, the sunlight would show it. The term *"eilikrines"* came to mean *"without wax."* The same word is translated **sincere** in Philippians. **That ye may approve things that are excellent; that ye may be sincere and without offence till the day of Christ; (Philippians 1:10)** Some pottery dealers would stamp their products *"sine cera"* ("without wax") as a pledge of quality. The Christian ought to be **sincere.** Peter is telling us that we need an unmixed, sincere, pure mind that will stand the test of the light of God's word.

There Must Be Remembrance

... by way of remembrance: That ye may be mindful of the words which were spoken before by the holy prophets, and of the commandment of us the apostles of the Lord and Saviour: (2 Peter 3:1c-2) We notice a great emphasis on remembering in this second epistle (2 Peter 1:12, 13, 15) One of the avenues of revival is the word of God. If we are not careful, even as God's people, we can forget and lose sight of the fact that our hope is in God rather than surrounding circumstances. Peter uses two words to describe our relationship to the word of God.

First, we see the word **remembrance** which simply means to *"recollect what you have heard." Second*, we are to be **mindful.** The word **mindful** carries the idea of setting the heart upon something. It is used here of fixing our heart upon the Word and applying it to our life. Paul said, **For they that are after the flesh do mind the things of the flesh; but they that are after the Spirit the things of the Spirit. (Romans 8:5)** Those who mind the things of the flesh are controlled and directed by the corrupt fallen nature. Their thoughts and affection are upon their own selfish interests. They seek their own gratification. They live for self. However, those who walk **after the Spirit** set their mind upon the word of God. They are concerned with His will for their lives. The priorities and principles of God are important to them. They are faithful in their Bible study, prayer, giving, attending Church, soul-winning, etc.

Notice that Peter uses the term **holy prophets**. He draws a sharp contrast between God's holy prophets and Satan's *unholy false prophets*. Next he says **... of the commandment of us the apostles of the Lord and Saviour.** Peter is speaking here of the word of God—he is drawing our attention to truth. He is calling upon believers to wake up to the truth of God's word. Though we live in uncertain times and apostasy surrounds us. Truth is under attack, wickedness is rampant and scoffers are bold to speak out. We nevertheless look to the word of God for it never changes, it is never wrong and it always offers hope for the child of God. **Thy word is very pure: therefore thy servant loveth it. (Psalm 119:140)** If we want a pure mind we must spend time in the pure word.

THE SCOFFER'S RIDICULE

Knowing this first, that there shall come in the last days scoffers... (2 Peter 3:3a) It's important that we keep the context in mind. In chapter 2 Peter dealt with the awful judgment that awaits the unbeliever with special emphasis on the false teachers. Notice that Peter prefaces his warning with words, **Knowing this first...** Peter is saying, *"Before we go any further you might as well get a hold of the fact they you are going to run into opposition. Accept the fact that there are going to be some people who reject your message."* In fact, he warns that they will not only reject our message, but some will make a sport out of ridiculing the message. He defines them as **scoffers.** Throughout the Bible, **scoffers** are those who ridicule and mock the things of God. Noah Webster says, *"... one who scoffs at religion, its ordinances and teachers, and who makes a mock of sin and the judgments and threatenings of God against sinners."* A scorner is one of the most dangerous men of Scripture. **Proud and haughty scorner is his name, who dealeth in proud wrath. (Proverbs 21:24)** These scoffers are prideful people who hate the truth. They boil with rage and will do anything to discredit God's word. Solomon warned, **He that reproveth a scorner getteth to himself shame: and he that rebuketh a wicked man getteth himself a blot. Reprove not a scorner, lest he hate thee: rebuke a wise man, and he will love thee. Proverbs 9:7-8** Trying to help a scorner is just inviting insult and shame. He is going to hate you for what you believe and he is going to come back at you with every kind of insult and mockery that he can muster up. Most of the time our attempts to help a scorner will be wasted. Our admonition and concern will only add to his scorning. It will give him more fuel for his fire. The scorner delights in ridiculing all who try to turn him from his folly. **A**

wise son heareth his father's instruction: but a scorner heareth not rebuke. Proverbs 13:1 A scorner refuses correction and help. Anyone who is dedicated to living for the Lord knows about scoffers and their ridicule. Peter tells us to expect such opposition.

The Scoffer's Conduct

... walking after their own lusts, (2 Peter 3:3b) The term walk is often used in Scripture to denote lifestyle. A man walks one course if he is a Pilgrim and another course if he is a settler. Peter ties their scoffing to their sinful desires. Because of their sin they hate the gospel. They want to live without any restraint.

Notice that these scoffers walk **after their own lusts.** They are traveling a course or a road that will get them to the desires of their flesh. All they are interested in is getting a little further down the road of pleasure. We live in a pleasure drunk society with all the partying, carousing, drunkenness, promiscuity and every kind of wickedness imaginable. Man has given in to his depravity and become a creature of the dark. Man is spiritually nocturnal. He loves the darkness. A lot of sinful activity takes place under the cover of darkness. There is something about the dark that gives sinners boldness. It seems to give a false sense of secrecy and security. You wonder why they scoff at us? It is because they have a lifestyle that they don't want to give up. They love their wickedness And they hate our light. The Bible says, **men loved darkness rather than light, because their deeds were evil. John 3:19** A person who is in love with sin will not receive the word of God. The Bible is a book of light—it sheds light on men's dark deeds and they hate it. May we as God's people in these last days stand as Moses did, **Choosing rather to suffer affliction with the people of God, than to enjoy the pleasures of sin for a season; (Hebrews 11:25)**

The Scoffer's Contempt

And saying, Where is the promise of his coming? for since the fathers fell asleep, all things continue as they were from the beginning of the creation. (2 Peter 3:4) Notice how they scornfully attack God's word. They say, **Where is the promise of his coming?** Notice their approach. They subtly question the word of God. They especially attack the doctrine of the Second Coming. They say, **... for since the fathers fell asleep, all things continue as they were from the beginning of the creation.** In other words, *"We have been hearing about the Second Coming and God's judgment all of our lives. Our fathers heard it all of their lives. Now they are dead and buried and everything just continues on as it always has."* Not only do they question the word of God, but the offer an argument against it. There is a great hatred of the Bible in our day. Their attack focuses foremost on trying to discredit the word of God. They are very subtle in their approach. They learned this from their father, the Devil.

Satan said to o Adam and Eve, **Yea, hath God said ... ? (Genesis 3:1)** The men of Malachi's day asked, **...Where is the God of judgment? (Malachi 2:17)** David's enemies asked, **...Where is thy God? (Psalm 42:3)** Jeremiah enemies asked, **... Where is the Word of the Lord... (Jeremiah 17:15)**

The Devil is a master deceiver and those who follow him know his tricks. They love to cast a shadow over God and His word. The implication in such questions is that God does not exist and the Bible is not true. They say, **Where is the promise of his coming?** Scoffers make the argument that since the promise of His coming has not been fulfilled, God does not keep His Word. The implication is that God's word can't be trusted. There is no hope for the Christian, no Heaven and God. Child of God! Learn your Bible! Don't let scoffers cast doubt on the Word of God.

The Scoffer's Creed

For this they willingly are ignorant of. (2 Peter 3:5a) Here is a simple fact. These scoffers are willingly ignorant. The issue is not that the scoffers are not simply uniformed, but they have purposefully shut their eyes to the truth. They willing ignore the evidence. It is interesting that Peter says creation is one of the things that **… they willing are ignorant of. For this they willingly are ignorant of, that by the word of God the heavens were of old, and the earth standing out of the water and in the water: (2 Peter 3:5)** The scoffers hate the Biblical account of creation. This is one of the reasons they worked so hard to kick the Bible out of schools and are working even harder to keep it out. By getting rid of creation their humanistic philosophy would be easier to peddle. Now the theory of evolution has infiltrated our schools, high-jacked our education, produced a generation of fools and saturated our land with a humanistic culture. Paul wrote, **Professing themselves to be wise, they became fools, And changed the glory of the uncorruptible God into an image made like to corruptible man, and to birds, and fourfooted beasts, and creeping things.**

(Romans 1:22-23) While rejecting revelation and denying God they profess themselves to be wise. They reject the fact of the Creator while all along they worship His creation. Divine revelation declares that, **In the beginning God created the heaven and the earth. (Genesis 1:1) By the word of the LORD were the heavens made; and all the host of them by the breath of his mouth. (Psalms 33:6)** Creation was according to the word of God. God spoke it and it came into existence. Ten times in Genesis chapter one we read the words, **God said.** No wonder Paul wrote, **Through faith we understand that the worlds were framed by the word of God, so that things which are seen were not made of things which do appear. (Hebrews 11:3)** God created the world by His word. Pseudo-Academia peddles all kinds of theories, but the bottom line is that God Almighty spoke the worlds into existence. He didn't use evolution! He didn't use the Big Bang! We are told that the things **...which are seen** [creation] **were not made of things which do appear.** There was nothing visible when God created the world. The word for **created** in **Genesis 1:1** is "*bara*" and means to create something out of nothing

Notice that they also choose to be ignorant of God's judgment in Noah's day. **Whereby the world that then was, being overflowed with water, perished: (2 Peter 3:6)** In Noah's day the scorners scorned and the mockers mocked at God's extended mercy. Day after day for 120 years the Spirit of God convicted them as Noah and his family prepared the ark. The Bible describes it as a time when **... once the longsuffering of God waited in the days of Noah, while the ark was a preparing... (1 Peter 3:20)** Just imagine the patience of God. But once the ark was finished God put

Noah and his family inside and unleashed His judgment on the wickedness of man. There is sufficient evidence to believe in God, but the infidel intelligentsia of our day hates God and His word so they ignore the facts and choose to be ignorant of the truth.

THE SAVIOUR'S RETRIBUTION

But the heavens and the earth, which are now, by the same word are kept in store, reserved unto fire against the day of judgment and perdition of ungodly men. (2 Peter 3:7) What a warning! Under inspiration of the Spirit of God Peter warns that the heavens and the earth that we now see are **...by the same word are kept in store.** The world exists today because God created it and His word keeps it. **And he is before all things, and by him all things consist. (Colossians 1:17)** Peter makes it clear that the same word that brought creation into existence and the same word that brought the world-wide flood of Noah's day will be the same word that brings judgment in the last days. It is a <u>Prophesied Word</u>, a <u>Proven Word</u> and a <u>Punishing Word</u>. Jesus said, **He that rejecteth me, and receiveth not my words, hath one that judgeth him: the word that I have spoken, the same shall judge him in the last day. (John 12:48)**

God Is Never Late
2 Peter 3:8-10

The rapture has been the blessed hope of God's people down through the ages. The Word of God declares that Christians in Rome, Corinth, Thessalonica, Philippi and Galatia were hopeful and waiting for the any moment return of Jesus Christ (1 Cor 15:50-58; 1 Thess 1:9-10; 4:13-18; 2:19; 5:23; Titus 2:13). The rapture is what we are looking for. **Looking for that blessed hope, and the glorious appearing of the great God and our Saviour Jesus Christ; (Titus 2:13)** The scoffers have no such hope, they despise our Lord's return. Peter answers the scoffers question, **Where is the promise of his coming?**

THE SCHEDULE OF HIS RETURN

But, beloved, be not ignorant of this one thing, that one day is with the Lord as a thousand years, and a thousand years as one day. (2 Peter 3:8) The return of Christ is scheduled and it is the next major event on God's prophetic time table. We see two important facts here.

Don't Forget About God's Truth

It is important for us to take notice of Peter's exhortation, **be not ignorant.** The word **ignorant** basically means *"to be uninformed"* or to *"lack knowledge."* The idea behind ignorant as it is used in our text is that of being ignorant about something due to forgetfulness. often have a problem with this. We sometimes get so wore out and weighed down that we forget all about God's grace and goodness and focus on our trials and troubles. Peter is admonishing us to keep our focus.

Don't Fret About God's Timing

We are reminded, **... that one day is with the Lord as a thousand years, and a thousand years as one day. (2 Peter 3:8b)** The scoffers look at the calendar and presume that Christ is not returning. However, believers look at the word of God and are assured of His glorious appearing. Moses in speaking about the power and providence of God said, **For a thousand years in thy sight are but as yesterday when it is past, and as a watch in the night. (Psalm 90:4)** God is never late. He is always right on time. He may seem slow to us because of the way we measure time but that is man's problem. God is not bound by our calendar. Our calendar starts over every January 1st, but God never starts eternity over. God operates in a different dimension than we do.

THE STRATEGY OF HIS RETURN

The Lord is not slack concerning his promise, as some men count slackness; but is longsuffering to us-ward, not willing that any should perish, but that all should come to repentance. (2 Peter 3:9) God has marvelous plans and is working according to those plans. Here Peter explains that God's promises can be trusted and the reason that He has not returned is due to His love for the lost.

God's Promise

The Lord is not slack concerning his promise, as some men count slackness. (2 Peter 3:9a) The word **slack** means to *"hesitate, linger, delay."* It carries the idea of loitering or loafing. God is not unfaithful concerning His promises. He is not loafing around with nothing to do. God has a plan and He is working that plan. He has not been Derailed! He has not been Detained! He has not been Delayed! He is not Dillydallying! He is 100% Dependable and we can count on His promises.

God's Patience

God **.... is longsuffering to us-ward (2 Peter 3:9b)** Longsuffering is a wonderful Bible word. The word simply means to suffer long. The modern translations mistakenly use the word patience here. But it is more than mere patience. One can be patient without suffering, but to be patient in suffering is a much greater task. **Longsuffering** comes from *makrothymeō*. It is a compound word made up of *makro* which means *"long,"* and *thymeō*, meaning *"temper."* The idea goes beyond mere patience and speaks of having patience under provocation. The Bible says that ... **God is angry with the wicked every day. (Psalm 7:11)** Sinners provoke God to judgment but He exercises patience and gives space for repentance. Longsuffering is one of God's great attributes. **But thou, O Lord, art a God full of compassion, and gracious, longsuffering, and plenteous in mercy and truth. (Psalm 86:15)**

God's Program

God is **...not willing that any should perish, but that all should come to repentance. (2 Peter 3:9c)** The word **willing** comes from *boulomai* and is used over thirty times in the New Testament. It carries the idea of being willing so far as desires go. God's desire is to save **all**. Not everyone will come to Christ but it is the desire of His heart to save all. Therefore, He is longsuffering, withholding His judgment,

Second Peter

desirous that many would be saved. During this dispensation our Lord has sent us out into the highways and the hedges to compel men to come in to the Marriage Supper of the Lamb (Luke 14:15-24). God will deal with the scoffers, but right now He is saving the lost. With God timing is always more important than time. Right now God is patiently allowing time to pass as He saves souls.

THE SWIFTNESS OF HIS RETURN

But the day of the Lord will come as a thief in the night... (2 Peter 3:10a) Notice the two words **will come**. There is absolute certainty in this statement. There is no question about it—judgment is coming. The Lord says that this event **will come as a thief in the night.** This is very descriptive of just how fast the day of the Lord will come upon the world. A thief does not call ahead and announce that he is coming to break into your house. He comes suddenly, robs you, and he is gone. There will be no further warning as to the day of the Lord. It will not be in the newspaper. It will not be written across the skies. God has spoken plainly through His word and through his people. God will without further warning snatch His Church from the earth and pour out His wrath upon the world. It will be Surprising, Swift, Sudden and Severe.

This analogy of a thief in the night applies only to the lost. God's people are not supposed to be taken by surprise. In fact we are to be aware of and looking for His return. **But of the times and the seasons, brethren, ye have no need that I write unto you. For yourselves know perfectly that the day of the Lord so cometh as a thief in the night. For when they shall say, Peace and safety; then sudden destruction** cometh upon them, as travail upon a woman with child; and they shall not escape. But ye, brethren, are not in darkness, that that day should overtake you as a thief. (1 Thessalonians 5:1-4)** God's people too often fall into the error of looking for signs. The fact is, we don't need a sign. We have His word and we walk by faith not by sight. We are not looking for signs, we are looking for our Saviour. Jesus said, **A wicked and adulterous generation seeketh after a sign; and there shall no sign be given unto it, but the sign of the prophet Jonas. And he left them, and departed. (Matthew 16:4)** The only thing we are to be looking for is the return of Christ. We are to be **looking for that blessed hope and the glorious appearing of the Lord and Saviour Jesus Christ. (Titus 2:13)** It is the unbelieving world that will be taken by surprise at the judgment of God. They have denied the Second coming. They have rejected the judgment of God. They have scorned God's people and mocked the truth. Just at the moment they least expect it, judgment will fall upon them. **For when they shall say, Peace and safety; then sudden destruction cometh upon them, as travail upon a woman with child; and they shall not escape. (1 Thessalonians 5:3)** Imagine the utter shock and fear that will grip the heart of the unbelieving world when these judgments fall. **But ye, brethren, are not in darkness, that that day should overtake you as a thief. (1 Thessalonians 5:4)** We are expecting it and watching for it.

THE SEVERITY OF HIS RETURN

*... **in the which the heavens shall pass away with a great noise, and the elements shall melt with fervent heat, the earth also and the works that are therein shall be burned up. (2 Peter 3:10b)** Here Peter describes the severity of the

day of the Lord. The day of the Lord is that period in which God pours out His fierce wrath upon the wicked. Some passages describing the day of the Lord are:

> Howl ye; for the <u>day of the lord</u> is at hand; it shall come as a destruction from the Almighty ... and they shall be afraid: pangs and sorrows shall take hold of them; they shall be in pain as a woman that travaileth: they shall be amazed one at another; their faces shall be as flames. (Isaiah 13:6-8)

> The great <u>day of the lord</u> is near, it is near, and hasteth greatly, even the voice of the <u>day of the lord</u>: the mighty man shall cry there bitterly. (Zephaniah 1:14)

> Blow ye the trumpet in Zion, and sound an alarm in my holy mountain: let all the inhabitants of the land tremble: for the <u>day of the lord</u> cometh, for it is nigh at hand. (Joel 2:1)

> The earth shall quake before them; the heavens shall tremble: the sun and the moon shall be dark, and the stars shall withdraw their shining: And the LORD shall utter his voice before his army: for his camp is very great: for he is strong that executeth his word: for the day of the LORD is great and very terrible; and who can abide it? (Joel 2:10-11)

> Enter into the rock, and hide thee in the dust, for fear of the LORD, and for the glory of his majesty. The lofty looks of man shall be humbled, and the haughtiness of men shall be bowed down, and the LORD alone shall be exalted in that day. For the <u>day of the LORD</u> of hosts shall be upon every one that is

proud and lofty, and upon every one that is lifted up; and he shall be brought low. (Isaiah 2:10-12)

Behold, the day of the LORD cometh, cruel both with wrath and fierce anger, to lay the land desolate: and he shall destroy the sinners thereof out of it. For the stars of heaven and the constellations thereof shall not give their light: the sun shall be darkened in his going forth, and the moon shall not cause her light to shine. (Isaiah 13:9-10)

This is an event also known as the wrath of the Lamb. It will be so terrible that men will beg for death. **And the kings of the earth, and the great men, and the rich men, and the chief captains, and the mighty men, and every bondman, and every free man, hid themselves in the dens and in the rocks of the mountains; And said to the mountains and rocks, Fall on us, and hide us from the face of him that sitteth on the throne, and from the wrath of the Lamb: For the great day of his wrath is come; and who shall be able to stand? (Revelation 6:15-17)** So severe will be the judgment of God that Jesus said, **And except those days should be shortened, there should no flesh be saved: but for the elect's sake those days shall be shortened. (Matthew 24:22)**

Peter tells us that **... the heavens shall pass away with a great noise, and the elements shall melt with fervent heat, the earth also and the works that are therein shall be burned up. (2 Peter 3:10c) Noise** is often associated with God's judgment. When the first seal is removed from the scroll at the beginning of the tribulation period there will be noise.

> And I saw when the Lamb opened one of the seals, and I heard, as it were the noise of thunder, one of the four beasts saying, Come and see. And I saw, and behold a white horse: and he that sat on him had a bow; and a crown was given unto him: and he went forth conquering, and to conquer. (Revelation 6:1-2)

Jeremiah spoke of the noise and roaring that would accompany the judgment of God.

> For, lo, I begin to bring evil on the city which is called by my name, and should ye be utterly unpunished? Ye shall not be unpunished: for I will call for a sword upon all the inhabitants of the earth, saith the LORD of hosts. Therefore prophesy thou against them all these words, and say unto them, The LORD shall roar from on high, and utter his voice from his holy habitation; he shall mightily roar upon his habitation; he shall give a shout, as they that tread *the grapes*, against all the inhabitants of the earth. A noise shall come *even* to the ends of the earth; for the LORD hath a controversy with the nations, he will plead with all flesh; he will give them *that are* wicked to the sword, saith the LORD. (Jeremiah 25:29-31)

> The LORD on high is mightier than the noise of many waters, yea, than the mighty waves of the sea. (Psalm 93:4)

Noise is very unsettling and often results in chaos and confusion. When God speaks and His judgment falls there is going to be mass confusion to go along with the collapse of society and carnage of the wicked.

We are told that **the elements shall melt with fervent heat, the earth also and the works that are therein shall be burned up.** Peter has already told us in verse 7 that God will use fire to destroy the heavens and the earth. Here he reiterates telling that **the elements shall melt with fervent heat** and everything **shall be burned up.** This is very graphic language describing the cataclysmic destruction of the universe. God is referred to in Scripture as a **consuming fire (Deuteronomy 4:24; 9:3, Hebrews 12:29)** There is coming a day when this old world that so many live for will be no more. This earth that so many worship will one day be consumed by the fire of God's judgment. Notice these verses.

> **The hills melted like wax at the presence of the LORD, at the presence of the Lord of the whole earth. (Psalms 97:5)**
>
> **The heathen raged, the kingdoms were moved: he uttered his voice, the earth melted. (Psalms 46:6)**
>
> **And the Lord GOD of hosts *is* he that toucheth the land, and it shall melt, and all that dwell therein shall mourn: and it shall rise up wholly like a flood; and shall be drowned, as *by* the flood of Egypt. (Amos 9:5)**
>
> **The mountains quake at him, and the hills melt, and the earth is burned at his presence, yea, the world, and all that dwell therein. (Nahum 1:5)**

Dr. Henry Morris writes:

> "Now, before the amazed John a vision is unfolded of an even grander scene than any he had ever witnessed before. In fact, the spectacle is so

blindingly glorious that the very earth itself disintegrates before it. The fire which had fallen from heaven to consume the multitudes following Gog and Magog seems to be nothing less than the unveiled glory, the pure, white hot energy, of the Creator in all His ineffable brilliance. Now that same cosmic power penetrates the very atomic structure of the earth and its atmosphere, and they are vaporized in a gigantic holocaust that brings this present world to an end."

As we study Bible prophecy we see that there are some terrible times to come for this unbelieving world. Not only will this world be destroyed, but God will also wipe it from our memory. **For, behold, I create new heavens and a new earth: and the former shall not be remembered, nor come into mind. (Isaiah 65:17)** This world is cursed and filled with sin. God is not going to allow the hurts, horrors and heartaches of this world to be with us for eternity.

According To His Promise
2 Peter 3:11-18

Peter says, **Nevertheless we, according to his promise, look for new heavens and a new earth, wherein dwelleth righteousness. (2 Peter 3:13)** Here is a wonderful promise. A blessed assurance. This promise sheds light on a dark situation. When Adam fell sin entered paradise resulting in God's curse upon this world. At that this world ceased to be what God had created it to be. However, we have the promise of new heavens and a new earth.

THE WALK OF THE SAINTS

Seeing then that all these things shall be dissolved, what manner of persons ought ye to be in all holy conversation and godliness, (2 Peter 3:11) The word **dissolved** refers back to verses 7-10 concerning the judgment of God and the destruction of the world. It comes form *lyō* and means *"to loose, untie, unleash."* The idea here is that of God unleashing His judgment on the world. Since judgment is coming Peter asks, **...what manner of persons ought ye to be in all holy conversation and godliness Looking for and hasting unto the coming of the day of God, wherein the heavens being on fire shall be dissolved, and the elements shall melt with fervent heat? (2 Peter 3:11b-12)** The word **manner** means *"of what sort."* The thought is what sort or what kind of a person am I. As we have already learned the word **conversation** speaks of lifestyle. Peter says that our lifestyle is to be **holy.** That is we are set apart from the world. We are in it, but not of it. This question challenges me to consider my lifestyle. Do I identify with the world that is going to be destroyed or does my lifestyle represent God and Heaven. That is a serious question to ponder.

THE WATCHFULNESS OF THE SAINTS

Nevertheless we, according to his promise, look for new heavens and a new earth, wherein dwelleth righteousness. (2 Peter 3:13) We are not looking for the destruction we are looking for a delivery. That is our hope. We are to be watching for our Lord to return in the rapture. Peter says, **according to his promise.** The return of Christ is as much a promise as any other promise of the Bible. This is something that we are to look for. Paul admonished the Thessalonian Church to **… to wait for his Son from heaven, whom he raised from the dead, even Jesus, which delivered us from the wrath to come. (1 Thessalonians 1:10)** The Scriptures continually admonish believers to **"watch," "be ready,"** and to expect His return **"at a time when ye think not."**

After the rapture of the Church God will begin to pour out His wrath upon the unbelieving world. This is the event known as the Tribulation period (Revelation 6-18). After this Jesus Christ will return to earth with His saints and establish His Millennial Reign (Revelation 19). Not long after the end of the Millennium this world will pass away and new one will take its place. John testified, **And I saw a new heaven and a new earth: for the first heaven and the first earth were passed away; and there was no more sea. (Revelation 21:1)** What a promise! What Satan ruined God will remake. We can count on His promises. **He is faithful that promised. (Hebrews 10:23)**

Wherefore, beloved, seeing that ye look for such things, be diligent that ye may be found of him in peace, without spot, and blameless. 2 Peter 3:14 This passage speaks of our diligence in looking for the return of Christ. The word diligent means to *"use speed, to be prompt or earnest, to be zealous."* It carries the idea of putting everything we have into living the Christian life and looking for His return. Peter says, **... that ye may be found of him in peace, without spot, and blameless.** The anticipation Christ's return has a purifying affect in our lifestyle. **Looking for that blessed hope, and the glorious appearing of the great God and our Saviour Jesus Christ; Who gave himself for us, that he might redeem us from all iniquity, and purify unto himself a peculiar people, zealous of good works. (Titus 2:13-14)** The imminent return of Jesus Christ motivates the believer to live a holy life and promotes the purity and separation of the Church from the world. This is our blessed hope. John said, **Beloved, now are we the sons of God, and it doth not yet appear what we shall be: but we know that, when he shall appear, we shall be like him; for we shall see him as he is. And every man that hath this hope in him purifieth himself, even as he is pure. (1 John 3:2-3)** The Christian's duty is to live at all times the way he would want his Saviour to find him living at the rapture.

THE WISDOM OF THE SAINTS

And account that the longsuffering of our Lord is salvation... (2 Peter 3:15a) The phrase **longsuffering of our**

Lord takes us back to verse 9 where Peter explained why the Lord delayed His return. Peter is reminding his readers that God is patient and longsuffering because He wants people to be saved. Peter goes on to say, **...even as our beloved brother Paul also according to the wisdom given unto him hath written unto you; As also in all his epistles, speaking in them of these things; in which are some things hard to be understood, which they that are unlearned and unstable wrest, as they do also the other scriptures, unto their own destruction. (2 Peter 3:15b-16)** Peter reminds his readers that Paul had taught the same truth in his letters. He says that although some of Paul's teachings are **things hard to be understood**, they are nevertheless **according to the wisdom given unto him** and just as authoritative as the rest of the Bible. Peter points out that the **unlearned and unstable wrest, as they do also the other scriptures, unto their own destruction.** The word wrest is from *strebloō* and means *"to distort, to twist, to pervert."* The wicked do everything in their power to twist and distort the Scripture.

THE WARNING TO THE SAINTS

Ye therefore, beloved, seeing ye know these things before, beware lest ye also, being led away with the error of the wicked, fall from your own stedfastness. (2 Peter 3:17) The word steadfastness comes from *stērigmos* meaning stability. It carries the idea of having a solid and sure footing. Even those who are stable and grounded in the faith need to be careful lest they be led into the error of the wicked. Paul warned, **Therefore, my beloved brethren, be ye stedfast, unmoveable, always abounding in the work of**

the Lord, forasmuch as ye know that your labour is not in vain in the Lord. (1 Corinthians 15:58)

THE WAY OF THE SAINTS

But grow in grace, and in the knowledge of our Lord and Saviour Jesus Christ. To him be glory both now and for ever. Amen. (2 Peter 3:18) The key to victory is spiritual growth. In his first letter Peter spoke on the subject of spiritual growth using the analogy of a newborn desiring milk. **As newborn babes, desire the sincere milk of the word, that ye may grow thereby. (1 Peter 2:2)** Peter uses the illustration of a newborn baby's hunger for milk to emphasize the believer's need to feed upon the word of God. Many believers fail to walk with God because they are Biblically illiterate. They are in such a condition because they neglect the study of God's word. David said, **Through thy precepts I get understanding: therefore I hate every false way. (Psalm 119:104)** David knew and despised the false ways because he was familiar with the precepts of God. Jesus said, **Ye do err, not knowing the scriptures. (Matthew 22:29)** The Bible is the spiritual food by which we grow in grace. If we are not a student of the word we will not be successful as a Christian.

www.ingramcontent.com/pod-product-compliance
Lightning Source LLC
Chambersburg PA
CBHW061638040426
42446CB00010B/1469